JUST SHOW UP!

God Can Use You

Encouraging vignettes of how God uses a life committed to serving Him.

Frank Garlock

MAJESTY MUSIC®

JUST SHOW UP!
God Can Use You

Editors: Shelly Hamilton, Karen Silos, Christianne Emory
Book layout: David Bonikowsky
Cover design: Dwight Reid

*A series of 34 vignettes emphasizing the One
Who can do more than we can even imagine, ask, or think
when we are committed to serving Him.*

*These accounts illustrate the fact that in many cases
we will probably not be aware of what God was doing at the time.
We learn some of the results much later.*

*The purpose of the book is to encourage, challenge, or inspire
any readers of these vignettes to use their talents and abilities
for the glory of God.*

Whatsoever ye do, do all to the glory of God.
—I Corinthians 10:31

Copyright © 2017 by Frank Garlock
fgmusicman@gmail.com
All rights reserved. Printed in USA.
ISBN: 978-0-9993546-0-5

Published by Sierra Creation
SierraCreation
www.sierracreation.com

O God, Thou hast taught me from my youth;
And hitherto have I declared Thy wondrous works.
Now also when I am old and grayheaded, O God,
Forsake me not,
Until I have shown Thy strength unto this generation,
And Thy power to every one that is to come.

Psalm 71:17-18

TABLE OF CONTENTS

PREFACE

I would like to begin the preface to this book by a quote from a close friend of mine, Dwight Gustafson, who is now with the Lord. Here is what he says about unplanned moments on page 17 of his book, *A Brighter Witness*:

> *"They happen only once. They can never be duplicated. But you were there . . . [God] reserves a few wonderful, unplanned moments to encourage us, to remind us of His faithfulness and loving care. We have all had them . . . those unexpected moments, dramatic intersections of ordinary life that glowed in the dark, when God's guidance was suddenly revealed."*

This book is about a number of those moments. Some of which are more than a half-century old.

Our small investment into the lives of others pays dividends that will last for eternity. Buildings don't last for eternity, schools don't last for eternity, but *people do*. As Dr. Bob Jones Sr. said many times: "we're clipping coupons" (referring to insurance policies that pay dividends.)

One of the main purposes of this book is to show what God can do when we let Him control our lives. He can "do exceeding abundantly above all that we ask or think" (Ephesians 3:20) "according to the riches of His glory" (verse 16) if we follow His leading. I am trusting that these vignettes will be like stone markers of God's goodness, similar to ones set up by men in the Bible: Noah, Abraham, Isaac, Jacob, to mention just a few. These "altars" show how God worked in my life to reveal His gracious hand and to remind me of His goodness in specific situations.

I would also like to include here a quote by C. H. Spurgeon since it exemplifies why I have chosen the title for this book. I believe it more closely resembles my own contemplation of my life with my Lord better than anything I could ever have said:

> *"As for myself, I am compelled to say with solemn truthfulness that I am not content with anything I have ever done. I have half wished to live my life over again, but now I regret that my proud heart allowed me so to wish, since the probabilities are that I should do worse the second time. Whatever grace has done for me I acknowledge with deep gratitude; but so far as I have done anything for myself, I beg pardon for it. I pray God to forgive my prayers, for they have been full of fault; I beseech Him to forgive even this confession, for it is not as humble as it ought to be; I beseech Him to wash my tears and purge my devotions and to baptize me into true burial with my Savior, that I may be quite forgotten in myself and only remembered in Him."*
> —*The Full Harvest*, page V.

When you read "Just Show Up!" remember that the Lord Jesus Christ *is* God, and *He* is the God Who wants to use you. As Colossians 1:16-17 says: "All things were created *by* Him and *for* Him . . . and *by Him all things consist.*" The only thing I did was strive to put my life in the hands of the One Who made me. My greatest desire is to let Him show me His love by working through me to bring glory to Himself.

INTRODUCTION

Flora Jean and I have just recently realized that between the two of us, we have 160 years of service for the Lord. We both were not only saved at five years of age, but Flora Jean began to play the piano in her small church in Okeene, Oklahoma at that same time. I began to play the trombone with my three siblings in churches at age five as well. Flora Jean and I were living 1,500 miles apart, but God was already working in each of our lives to prepare us to serve Him together. Although we presently do not know what the future holds, we firmly believe He is not through using us yet.

I have sought to bring some chronology to the events in this book, however, the time frames are intertwined and overlap. These stories are only related in that they have demonstrated to me that God is interested in every little facet of our lives. Everything about our beings substantiates the fact that God not only controls the macrocosm (the sun and the planets as well as the gigantic galaxies with their billions of stars), but He also is involved in and presides over the microcosm as well.

God's creation of trillions of grains of sand is an example of his interest in the small things. When magnified 250 times, sand grains are revealed to be like snowflakes. No two are alike! There is an infinite variety of their shapes and colors. Some look like precious gems, some resemble yellow and brown eggs, some are square, some are spherical, some are flat, and some even look like icicles [see figure 1].

Another example of God's presiding over the microcosm can be found in our DNA. Each one of our eyes has 107,000,000 (that's one hundred seven million) cells, and each one of these cells contains the entire DNA that is unique to each one of us. Our nerve cells are also highly individual. No two cells are exactly the same. Each neuron is unique in all the universe. Christ tells us in Matthew 10:30 that "the very hairs of your head are all numbered." God is concerned and involved in all the minute things of our lives.

As you read this book, remember what the Bible says about Ruth in Ruth 2:3. God tells us it just happened, "her hap," that she gleaned in the field of Boaz. In fact, that entire book of Ruth is about how God orchestrated every detail in her life. All the main characters of the book just showed up to witness what God was doing *for* them and *through* them. God delights in starting with nothing (a Moabite in this case) to accomplish His will (she is in the line of Christ—Matthew 1:5).

Flora Jean and I regularly marvel at what God has allowed us, two of His most unworthy servants, to do for Him. As Ruth says in speaking to Boaz: "Why have I found grace in thine eyes, that thou shouldest take knowledge of me?" (Ruth 2:10) In our case, God took a poor city boy (read *I, Being in the Way* to see how poor I was) and a country girl (she milked cows and plucked chickens), and by His grace used us for His glory. In thinking back over the last 65 years, we astonishingly say that the God of the universe loved us so much that He brought together a "city-slicker" and a "country bumkin" from different backgrounds and different parts of the country to accomplish His will.

VIGNETTE 1

FAITHFUL SERVANTS

ONE OF the blessings of serving the Lord is the way He brings faithful servants across your path who become your friends for life. One of those faithful servants is Dr. Bob Shelton whom Flora Jean and I have known and have been friends with for over 67 years now. Bob was one year ahead of me when we were students at Bob Jones University in 1949.

As a very young student at BJU, I was impressed with Bob right away. He was not only a student leader, talented both as a preacher and a singer, but he was also a spiritual leader as well. He and I went on what was called "extension" in those days to many churches all over the Southeast. He had a beautiful voice, and we combined our voices with other young men to form quartets that ministered on and off the campus of the university.

In 1951, the year that Flora Jean and I began to date, Chang Kai-shek was asking for preachers and evangelists to reach 500,000 of his soldiers with the gospel. These soldiers were in Taiwan because they had been driven out of China by the communists. Dr. Bob Jones Sr. received the request and decided to send some of his "preacher boys" over to Taiwan to reach those soldiers. Bob put off his scheduled wedding with Nancy to answer that call.

Bob and the other men who went to fulfill that mission won over 100,000 of those soldiers to the Lord. All 100,000 of those men took and completed the Navigators Bible Study Course, requiring a year of study and memorization. I recently asked Bob if it is possible that some of the "Underground Church" in China today could have come from some of those men who went back to China and spread the gospel in that needy, communist country. He said that could possibly be true. This is just another example of how God works when we are faithful to serve Him wherever He places us.

After a preaching tour in the Pescadores, a chain of islands halfway between Taiwan and Mainland China, Bob and Nancy were married on January 3, 1953. They went to Okinawa and then to Vietnam in 1957, thinking this would be their life's ministry. However, they had to leave Vietnam in 1961 as the Viet Cong were taking over 80% of the country.

The Sheltons' next ministry was in 1962 when Bob became pastor of his home church in Pontiac, Michigan. This church, First Baptist of Pontiac, was where Dr. H. H. Savage had been pastor for thirty-eight years.

Flora Jean and I have been in meetings with the Sheltons over the years. We were privileged to do their special music at a New Year's Eve service at First Baptist. While he was there, Dr. Shelton began his own radio ministry. This radio broadcast continues to this day (2017), reaching the world with an emphasis on Bible prophecy that is so necessary as the Lord's return seems imminent.

I would suggest reading three books that Dr. Shelton has written. The first book, about his varied ministries for over 60 years, is called *Through a Great Door*. The next two books are about Bible prophecy and are called *God's Prophetic Blueprint* and *Prophecy in Context*. These well-written and informative books will challenge you and bless your heart.

VIGNETTE 2

ONE MAN'S INFLUENCE ON A BOY

WHEN FLORA Jean and I went to Brent Baptist Church in Pensacola, Florida in 1954, I was only 23 years old. Since I was young, many of the teenagers in the church were not far behind me in age. Most of those "kids" are now in their 70's, and some of them have already turned 80. They are still my "kids" that I taught, worked with, and loved in the years that I was at Brent.

During the three and one-half years that I was there, I know of 14 of these kids who are serving the Lord in what we call "full-time service." Dr. Nicky Chavers was among that unique group of young people. Here is his testimony:

> When I was 10 years old, I began my own live television program called "Songs by Nicky Chavers." It was a fifteen-minute show during which I sang a variety of music. This unusual opportunity was one of several early indications that God had His hand on me. He had begun preparing me for a public ministry. The thing I liked the most was singing in churches. That is where I felt the presence of God, and my mother had taught me: "Nicky, what you have is a gift. It was given to you by the Lord. Always use your gifts for Him."
>
> A few years later, I was asked to sing at a Baptist church. The occasion was a talent contest organized by the new 24-year-old music director, Frank Garlock. I did not know

it then, but God was leading me to meet someone very special who would change my life. I was in awe of this young music director, a graduate of Bob Jones University. He and his wife, Flora Jean, were extremely talented and dedicated, and since I had had little formal training in music, their classes in music theory, their training in choral music, instrumental music, and vocal ensembles really attracted me.

What a blessing it was to develop a new philosophy of music under Frank Garlock and to begin to understand the Bible and God's will for my life. I attribute the spiritual direction of my life to godly teachers, but to Frank Garlock I must attribute the musical, artistic, and philosophical direction of my life. I have never seen anyone before or since who made such an impact on people through music and a biblical philosophy of life. When I was a boy in Pensacola, Florida, I saw him and his wife take a choir that was nothing, and in a matter of months turn it into a functioning choral group, singing choruses from Handel's Messiah.

However, early into the second semester of my senior year in high school, tragedy struck the ministry of Brent Baptist Church. The church split and our Christian school closed. I prayed about what to do. I did not feel that God would have me go back into a secular humanist environment. The only other Christian high school I knew was over 500 miles away—Bob Jones Academy in Greenville, SC. I had visited the campus once at Thanksgiving time and loved it. That's where I believed God wanted me to go.

Because they knew God's hand was on me, the teachers at Brent Christian School got together and decided to pay my way to Bob Jones Academy. They called Greenville to get me in, but they were told that it was impossible. Registration was closed and the school was already four weeks into the semester. The teachers urged Bob Jones to make an exception for me.

I later learned that in an administrative conference at Bob Jones University, there had been a discussion on whether to allow me to attend the Academy. Dr. Bob Jones Sr., who in those days almost never went to administrative conferences, walked in and sat down. He was the Founder of both the University and the Academy. Dr. Bob asked what they were discussing, and he was given the details of the case. He took it all in and then said, "Let the boy come." What could the administrators say? The Founder had said, "Let the boy come." A phone call was made, and I packed my bags.

However, the man who was to take me to Greenville that night after a church service had some problems and couldn't take me. So my mother took me downtown to the bus station. With a tearful kiss, she put me on a Greyhound bus for Greenville, South Carolina at midnight. I was a senior in high school; but as the bus sped through the night, I cried almost all the way to Bob Jones.

Unknown to me, the Garlocks had finished grad school at Eastman and had joined the faculty at Bob Jones. My second day on campus, I had quite a surprise. I saw Frank Garlock walking toward me on the sidewalk. "Brother

Frank!" [Vignette 6.] I cried out and ran toward him, my arms outstretched.

Even though I was only a high school senior, he took me right into his Vesper choir, and I might add—right into his heart. The next five years could be described as launching out into the educational deep; and when storms came, the Garlocks were my anchor. Besides being my constant counselor, he taught me music theory, choral conducting, choral writing and arranging, and 16th century counterpoint. I was in his Vesper choir for five years. I also sang in his men's quartet and church choir at the church where he was the music minister, Southside Baptist Church.

At Southside, he had a hundred-voice choir, which sang some of their specials from memory. He had a 24-piece orchestra, a trombone choir, ladies groups, and 16 singing men all ministering through excellent sacred music, much of which Dr. Garlock wrote himself. At his side, Flora Jean accompanied the choir, special groups and played innumerable original piano offertories—in quality and complexity never equaled in church music.

One of the most unusual things I ever saw Dr. Garlock do (though I am sure it was not hard for him to do it!) was to turn the 2,500 member congregation at Southside Baptist Church into a huge choir. He would write a special arrangement of some sacred classic that most people were at least familiar with and arrange the accompaniment for his university trombone choir. After dividing the whole congregation into soprano, alto, tenor, and bass sections, he would have a congregational rehearsal one Sunday evening and then a celebration the next Sunday evening.

For these special services, the congregation would sometimes swell to well over 3,000, as people came just to hear the congregation sing as a huge choir. The balcony would be packed, and there would be chairs in every aisle. You have never heard anything like it! I have never heard of another church in America even attempting such a thing. Of course, they did not have Frank and Flora Jean Garlock.

After I graduated from Bob Jones and joined the faculty, I had the privilege of working with Dr. Garlock for two years on dozens of vesper programs. Our creative spirits fed each other, and the college students seemed to appreciate our efforts to make vespers exciting and inspiring. His choir was always superb, his special groups sang as one voice, and his 26-member trombone choir filled Rodeheaver Auditorium with the classics of sacred music.

In all these associations with Dr. Garlock as teacher, conductor, composer, arranger, collaborator, minister, and friend—he was pumping into me a musical and spiritual philosophy that remains with me to this day. Many of the techniques I use in writing and directing plays for the Academy of Arts, and assuredly my skills in conducting and composition, can be traced back to his influence.

My wife and I founded *The Academy of Arts* in 1971 to make the Bible "come alive" for people. I had observed that most people do not read the Bible, and many of the ones who do read it do not read it with any degree of understanding. I also observed that drama had had a significant influence on people in the US through the movie industry.

I had double majored in Bible and Sacred Music and had a minor in speech. Then I had completed a Master's degree in Music and Dramatic production. During my tenure at Bob Jones, I had trained opera choruses and oratorio choruses for Dr. Gustafson, Dean of the School of Fine Arts. I had also been in a number of Shakespearean plays and had done a lot of directing.

In short I had seen the effectiveness of drama and music in productions, and I felt that by this medium the average person could be given a fresh appreciation for the Bible. So, in 1971 we took out our first drama team. This drama team performed in 56 churches that summer. We saw 40 people trust Christ and over 200 decisions of dedication. People kept saying to us: "It just makes the Bible come alive." So we took that as our motto for the drama team ministry.

The next year we took out two drama teams, and every year after that we have taken out three teams, ministering each summer to some 25,000 people. More than 1,600 young people have traveled on one of our teams, and more than a million people have seen "the Bible come alive" over the years.

In 1973, the Christian school movement was going strong, and we saw an opportunity to minister to the thousands of young people who had left public schools and were now in these schools. I felt a kinship with these young people because when I was growing up in Pensacola, Florida, I had always looked forward to going to the large Pensacola High School. I wanted to be a part of their excellent fine arts program. However, I had been taken out of the public school system and had been placed in a small Christian school which offered almost none of these opportunities. So The Academy of Arts began week-long drama seminars for Christian schools. We called them "Instant Drama" seminars—because all you add is people. We supplied everything else—the costumes, the props, the scenery, the stage lights, and a team of qualified people to direct a Christian or biblical drama.

Since 1973, The Academy of Arts has conducted more than 1,800 of these drama seminars in Christian schools and home school groups, directly involving more than 90,000 young people and performing for more than 700,000 people.

In the early 2000s The Academy of Arts purchased an old school for $1 per square foot. After extensive renovations on the 21,000 square foot structure, the ministry moved into that building in 2007. Now, in this new facility, we have beautiful offices, restrooms, dormitories, make-up rooms, rehearsal rooms, a greenroom, a cafeteria and a 400-seat auditorium, which we dubbed "The Logos Theatre."

In 2008, my wife and I went into semi-retirement and turned the ministry over to our daughter, Nicole and her husband, Noah Stratton. Under their excellent leadership, the ministry has risen to heights we only imagined before.

The Academy of Arts now trains its teams, runs a Christian Conservatory, conducts Drama Camps, Music Camps, Film Camps and performs in the Logos Theatre for thousands of people from the Greenville area each year. Nicole Stratton was recently recognized by the South Carolina Senate with a resolution of commendation for her contributions to the fine arts in the upstate. Along with this recognition was a letter from the Governor, commending her for her accomplishments.

What I have said here about Dr. Garlock's influence on me, my family, and on my ministry, could be multiplied a thousand times by men and women all over America and on the mission field. If these servants of God who are all over the globe were given the opportunity, they would echo what I have said; and some could say even more!

Dr. Bob Jones Sr. used to say, "Every great man I ever knew came, at one time, under the dominating power of a great truth." That saying not only fits Frank Garlock, for he lived under the dominating power of many great truths, but it also fits those to whom he ministered. He himself burned many great truths into the hearts of thousands, and none of us will ever forget them!

—*Dr. Nicky Chavers*

VIGNETTE 3

A Sixty-Year Friendship

FLAY AND Margaret Allen are two of the quintessential examples of the title and subtitle of this book. They have watched God work on the mission fields where the Lord called them (Mexico, Chile, and Spain) as they showed up to do whatever God wanted them to do in each country. What Flay has written for this vignette is just a small sample of all that the Lord allowed them to be for Him.

Of all the friends I have had over the years, no man has ever been closer to being a brother to me than Flay Allen. Perhaps it is because we both started from such humble backgrounds; or perhaps it is because we both marvel that God has chosen to use each of us; or perhaps it is because we both love music and have a desire to use it for the Lord wherever He has called us.

Beyond that, I believe there is another characteristic that God has given both Flay Allen and me, and that is an overriding desire to *encourage others* to become all that God wants them to be. In the Scripture, the Greek word for this God-given gift is *paraklesis*, and it refers to someone who wants to come alongside others to help them be successful. It is sometimes called the Spiritual gift of *encouraging*, *exhortation, comfort,* or *consolation*—as is the case with Barnabas in Acts 4:36 in his relationship with the Apostle Paul. Flay is always encouraging others, including me. Here is Flay Allen's testimony:

My musical family grew up in the hills of North Carolina, totally immersed in country and bluegrass music. My three brothers and I each learned to play a couple of stringed instruments, "by ear" of course. During my high school years, we participated in Saturday radio programs on two local stations. We also competed in all the "Fiddler's Convention" contests. Back in those days, I believe all four of us had our eyes secretly turned toward Nashville.

When my pastor, Gene Fisher, convinced me to study at Bob Jones University after high school, it never occurred to me to try for a music major. I knew that they promoted "highfalutin" classical music down there.

In 1955 when I was 21 and after two and a half years at the university, I stayed out of the university for a year due to financial difficulties and worked in construction in Pensacola, Florida. My first serious challenge to develop my musical talents came from Frank Garlock who was then the music director at Brent Baptist Church in Pensacola. Frank evidently saw something in me of which I was un-aware. He immediately invited me to join his church choir. He was rapidly building a music program there so he started giving me trombone lessons. When he announced a class for those who wanted to lead congregational sing-ing, I signed up. His wife, Flora Jean, also gave me voice lessons. Before the year was over, Frank even made me his assistant choir director.

Frank pushed me into learning to read music. He told me, "You've got enough *ear* for two people, but that alone will often let you down. You need to learn how music is con-structed, and that involves what is called music theory." After an exciting and profitable year, I returned to Bob

Jones University to complete my degree. Even though I would have loved to study more music, I realized it was too late to change my major. I graduated in 1958 with a degree in humanities. Margaret, my beautiful wife who was also very talented in music, and I were married in 1959.

In 1960, we started our first term of missionary service in Mexico. We became part of a missionary evangelistic team. Imagine my surprise when the leader of our team said, "Flay, you have had more musical training than the rest of us. You will be responsible for preparing special musical arrangements for our evangelistic campaigns as well as our weekly radio broadcasts."

With the Lord's help, I made a serious effort to make and prepare arrangements. But Frank was right. Time after time my "ear" let me down. Margaret and I prayed about it, and after three years—I told the team, "I'm going back to BJU to major in music!"

When we got back to Greenville, I discovered that Frank Garlock had completed his studies at the Eastman School of Music and had returned to BJU to be the head of the Music Theory department.

Even though I had a weak musical background, I was accepted into the program. After one semester, I enrolled in Dr. Garlock's sophomore music theory class. Looking back on that experience, I would have to say that I was probably the least prepared of all the music majors who entered his class. I believe, however, that my enthusiasm and unawareness enabled me to carry my ignorance with blissful dignity. I remember that I tried to stay quiet and smile a lot.

During one of our late night church brass quartet rehearsals, I was having a hard time reading my trombone part. Frank dismissed the other two players and worked with me for about a half hour on my sight-reading. That night, he told me, "I have always been willing to go to the mission field, but I am convinced that God has not called me to do that." Then he added, "If I can spend some extra time helping people like you who are going, I feel that I can multiply my influence for the Lord around the world." (I personally know several of his "music students" who are making a big difference for the Lord in Europe as well as Central and South America.)

Folks, the Lord enabled me to earn a degree in Music Education. I can't remember my exact grade point average, but I believe I graduated "Magna Cum Lucky!" Several years later, with Dr. Garlock's encouragement, I earned a Master's of Music degree in Sacred Music in choral conducting.

Now as I look back over 52 years on the mission field, I realize that many of the greatest opportunities for service the Lord gave me were in the area of music. I have had the privilege of directing music or participating in sacred music seminars in more than a dozen countries.

With Dr. Garlock's encouragement, Margaret and I moved to Mexico in 1998 for two years where we set up the music department for the Christian University of the Americas in Monterrey.

Our Spanish team has produced several sacred recordings. (The Garlocks came to Spain and helped us on four recordings and one in the USA.) We have also published several volumes of Majesty Music cantatas and choral arrangements.

With the help of Dr. Garlock and Frank Buie, president of our mission board, Faith Christian Missions, we had the privilege of publishing a 600-page Spanish hymnbook named *Himnos Majestuosos*. It is now in its fourth printing.

I would have to say that my serious "musical journey" started with Frank Garlock in 1955. Even this year (sixty years later), Dr. Garlock and I have had invitations for music seminars in Argentina, Chile, Peru, and Costa Rica.

Last of all, I thank the Lord for the wonderful opportunities of service that He has given Margaret and me. In addition to that, I thank my dear friend, Frank Garlock, for guiding and encouraging me all along this sixty-year musical journey. I greatly treasure the friendship we have had for all those years!

—Flay Allen

There are four things I need to add to what Flay has written.

1. He neglected to tell you that he is now the director of Faith Christian Missions with 24 missionaries on the field.

2. He also didn't tell you that Puerto Rico Baptist College gave him an honorary doctoral degree in sacred music in 2000 and that his alma mater, Bob Jones University, gave him an honorary Doctor of Divinity degree at the commencement exercises in 2015.

3. He omitted the fact that he has written a book recounting stories from his ministry around the world. *The Joy of Missions: 50 Years of Ministry Seen from the Lighter Side* was published by CTS Publications in 2016.

4. He also failed to mention that he regularly tells people that he was my favorite student in Sophomore Music Theory because I invited him to be in the class a second year. (The real story is that I realized his weak background and believed that he needed more of what that course offered if he were going to be an effective music minister on the mission field.) By the way, Flay has been a very effective and influential musical missionary ever since he returned for his Music Education degree in 1963, 52 years ago.

VIGNETTE 4

A DIVINE APPOINTMENT

GETTYS ALLEN is a younger brother of Flay Allen, the missionary who wrote the previous vignette, "A Sixty-Year Friendship." As you read what Gettys has written, it would be worthwhile for you to read again about the Allen family's humble beginnings in North Carolina. To me, the life of this faithful music director is just another illustration that God seems to delight in taking a simple piece of clay and molding a masterpiece in order to accomplish His will. The following is the testimony of J. Gettys Allen:

> I was attending college in the mid 50s and made a visit to Pensacola, Florida to visit my sister, Violet Allen, a teacher at Brent Christian School. I attended a church service at Brent Baptist Church that weekend and experienced a demonstration of God's power and presence in the service that overwhelmed me. The vibrant music by the church choir, orchestra, and congregation under the direction of Frank Garlock was exhilarating. That experience stirred a desire in my heart to use the musical talents which God had given me to serve Him if given the opportunity to do so. Although I was not a music major in college, I did take several elective music courses to better equip me for future service.

> After college I joined the military service and was sent to Berlin, Germany. I became part of the choir at a base chapel. The choral director was a civilian from the USA doing

research for a doctoral degree in music. He completed his studies about a month after I arrived in Berlin and returned to the States in order to complete his doctoral dissertation. We had an excellent choir and began searching for a new director. Eventually, I was asked to direct it; and it was one of the highlights of my stint in the army.

Upon my return to the States and to civilian life, I moved to Pensacola, Florida and was employed by Pensacola Christian School. Shortly after my arrival, I was approached by the church pianist at Brent Baptist Church. She indicated that the current music director would be leaving in a few weeks and wondered if I would have an interest in becoming the church music director. Incidentally, this is the same church where I first met Dr. Garlock. He had left the church several years earlier to pursue additional musical studies in New York. Fortunately, there were some wonderful musicians in the choir and orchestra who had been trained by the Garlocks. Needless to say, I gladly accepted the opportunity.

I began taking additional music courses at a local college and university in order to help me to be more effective as a church music director. Several years later I had the privilege of earning a graduate degree in music with a proficiency in conducting under the direction of Dr. Garlock.

I believe in divine appointments, and I am convinced that meeting Dr. Garlock 60 years ago was not a serendipitous event. I never anticipated becoming a church music director, but God brings people and events into our lives to direct our paths in the way that we should go. Thanks to God and to my friend and mentor Dr. Frank Garlock, I have been a church music director for 55 years. I currently direct the nationally televised "Rejoice Choir" of the Campus Church of Pensacola Christian College and have done so for the past 41 years.

In addition to my music ministry with the Campus Church, I also conduct choral seminars and direct the music for various conferences. I also direct the Azalea Trace community chorus for annual Spring and Christmas concerts. God has truly given me many opportunities to serve Him through music for which I am thankful. *To God Be the Glory*!!!

—J. Gettys Allen

I would like to add to this vignette a letter from a friend who is the older sister of both Flay and Gettys Allen. She wrote to Flora Jean just recently. The sister's name is Violet Allen, and Flora Jean and I have known her since 1955 when she became one of the teachers at Brent Christian School in Pensacola where I was the novice principal.

You have read about her in several of these vignettes without realizing that it was Violet that you were reading about. For instance, in Vignette 2, it was Violet who undertook the responsibility of paying Nicky Chavers' way for him to attend Bob Jones Academy.

In Vignette 3, Violet was the one who encouraged Flay to return to Bob Jones University and complete the training he needed to be all that God wanted him to be. She also helped to pay his way. In Vignette 4, Violet was one of the people who encouraged Gettys to "stay with the stuff," not get discouraged over the disappointments that come to all music directors, and to become the effective choir director that he is today.

Here is what Violet wrote to Flora Jean:

> *"I wanted to let you know my thoughts and prayers are with you daily. You and Frank have been a special blessing to all of my immediate family since I first met you in the early fifties. Frank has been a special help and encouragement to my brothers with their love of music and encouraged them to be a testimony in their choices. Thank you both for loving the Lord and for being a testimony for Him as long as we have known you. Because of you both, my four brothers have all loved good music, and three of my brothers have been music directors in churches for many years."*

Violet is one of those people who likes to stay in the background, but she has been the "unseen encourager" behind many missionaries mentioned in this book as well. This faithful servant of the Lord is one of those people who I believe will, as we stand before the Lord, receive His "well done." I cannot help but be reminded of what Fanny Crosby's tombstone says: "She hath done what she could!" I believe Violet's prayers are one of the reasons God has done so much for Flora Jean and me as we have served the Lord for the last 60 years.

VIGNETTE 5

Special Friends

I HAVE always said that when you are in "the ministry," you usually don't get to have many close friends—but you do need some! God has been so good to me over the years to have four men that I consider special, close friends. Three of them have written vignettes for this book—Flay Allen in "A Sixty-year Friendship;" Kurt Woetzel in "A Profound Impact;" and Ron Hamilton in "Daddy, Who Is that Boy?"

For this vignette, I want to mention another man who has been "closer than a brother" for over 54 years: a man known by many as Major Ron Brooks. Ron had served in the U.S. Army and then went to BJU as a student. The Brooks, like many of the rest of us, did not have much money. But as soon as we met, they invited us over to the place they were living for pizza after church one Sunday evening. We were delighted to go, but we wondered why they served *coffee* with pizza. It wasn't until we had known them for quite a while that we learned they had stretched one grocery-bought pizza into two small pizzas, and the only thing they had in the house to go with the pizza was coffee. They could not even afford a soft drink.

This, however, began a close relationship that has lasted until this day. It would take a book much larger than this one to tell of all the things that the Brooks and the Garlocks have done together over the years, but here is how the Brooks describe our 54-year relationship:

We first met the Garlocks in April, 1961, at Southside Baptist Church. Our friendship has grown over the years, and we are not only best friends—we are family. Not many people can say they have had such close friends for over 50 years. Praise the Lord, the Brooks and Garlocks can say that.

After Ron's graduation from Bob Jones University, we served there together on the faculty. In 1967-68 and 1971-72, when Ron was recalled and sent to Vietnam, Frank and Flora Jean were a great help to Barbara and our children. Several years later we served together on the church staff at Southside Baptist Church.

Our friendship had to span the ocean when we went to Germany in February 1987 to plant a church for American Military families. We were the first from the States to minister in a new church plant in Heidelberg. The Garlocks came to visit us in June that year, and when God called us back to the United States in November 1990, the Garlocks flew to Germany to help us pack. In January 1991, when Ron became a Field Director for Baptist World Mission, they drove to Alabama to help us unpack. We would call that a close friendship.

Through the years we have celebrated anniversaries together, vacationed together, and made mission trips together. We have studied the Bible together and encouraged each other to keep serving the Lord. Our families have spent the holidays cooking and eating together. We even had the privilege of living close together several times and enjoyed being together several times a week. These are our backdoor friends, our come as you are or come as we are friends, and our comfortable friends. We have been there for each other through joy and sorrow, through laughter and tears.

Frank and Flora Jean Garlock have developed and used their God given musical talents to bless and encourage untold numbers of Christians worldwide. Frank learned Spanish in his elder years so he could better minister to Spanish speaking Christians. A talented musician, songwriter, and spirit-filled preacher and teacher—these terms best describe this friend and example of a dedicated Christian. We are glad to still call the Garlocks dear friends. Our forever friends!

—*Ron and Barbara Brooks*

I want to add an aspect of our relationship with the Brooks that has knit our hearts together in an unusual but important way. The four of us, Ron and Barbara and Flora Jean and I have spent many hours discussing spiritual things and comparing Scripture with Scripture. The Bible, in Proverbs 27:17, says that "iron sharpeneth iron; so a man sharpeneth the countenance of his friend." Therefore, these special times have enriched the lives of all four of us.

Let me illustrate that last paragraph. One Sunday night, we met with the Brooks and another couple after the Sunday evening service at church. It wasn't long into the discussion of biblical principles that the other couple said: "Do you always talk like this?" To the astonishment of our guests, all four of us answered in the affirmative!

I don't believe any man has had better friends than the four men I have mentioned in this vignette. (I should also mention that the wives of these four have also been close friends.) Again, God worked on our behalf in all the places He has put Flora Jean and me. He has brought special friends to encourage and help us to serve the Lord. I look forward to the day when we will all be in heaven and will have eternity to look back and rejoice over all that God did while we were here on this earth.

Ron Brooks went to be with the Lord on January 11th of 2016. He wrote this vignette almost exactly two months before he went home to glory! "We'll see you soon, dear friend!"

VIGNETTE 6

BROTHER FRANK

YOU WILL notice in these next testimonies from Al and Helga Bonikowsky that they refer to me as "Brother Frank." That was the name that Pastor Dolphus Price gave me when I went to Brent Baptist Church in Pensacola, Florida in 1954. This term of affection has been my favorite designation ever since. To this day, most of our missionary friends primarily know me as "Brother Frank."

My purpose for including testimonies from missionaries in this book stems from the fact that although God never "called" Flora Jean and me to the mission field, a large part our ministry has been to support missions. Our trips overseas to 50 countries have all involved missionary work. God has also allowed us to raise money for missionary projects that encompass many parts of the world, including some countries that we have never even visited.

There is no way that we in our own strength could have raised the amounts of money that were involved. Once again God used us, and all we did was show up to encourage God's people to do for those, like Al and Helga, who were sacrificing so much.

Flora Jean and I have been privileged to know people like the Bonikowskys, the Allens [Vignette 3], and the Flowers [Vignette 26] let alone count them as some of our dearest friends. I have decided to include the stories of Al and Helga separately since they are each so unique.

From Al:

Our relationship with Brother Frank and his wife, Flora Jean, goes all the way back to 1968 when we, as missionary candidates, arrived in Greenville, South Carolina to attend Bob Jones University. The main thing that drew us to Southside Baptist Church in Greenville was the outstanding music program which the Garlocks were in charge of. Frank directed both the choir and the congregational singing, and Flora Jean complemented his direction with her competent piano accompaniment.

The exceptionally proficient singing of the choir made us think the singers were all professionals even though they all were just ordinary church members. In addition, there was a group of twelve men, that I would call a "triple quartet," that sang regularly in the services. They were always a blessing as they sang every song from memory. Each time we returned to the United States on furlough from Spain, the music at Southside made us think we were listening to something celestial. This always "recharged our spiritual batteries" and helped us to remain faithful to our calling in the difficult Basque region of northern Spain.

Music has always played a special part in the lives and ministries of my family. My grandfather, Emil Bonikowsky, was a preacher in Russia, the Ukraine, and Poland during the years before and after the First World War—which is 100 years ago. During several years of exile in Siberia, sixteen children were born into his family. Many of my grandfather's children became preachers in both the United States and Canada where I was born.

Brother Frank was and is my inspiration for good sacred music. Frank's solo album called "My Life Is Thine" remains my favorite source of inspiration to this day. We have passed that on to our children and grandchildren—so that Andy, who is also a missionary to the Basque region of Spain, and Andy's two sons, David and Danny, are also using music as a part of their ministries in that same part of the world where God called us 42 years ago.

In God's timing, He has allowed much of the music of the Garlocks to be translated into Spanish so that people who speak that language can enjoy and receive a blessing from good, conservative, traditional music that exalts the Lord and brings glory to Him.

—*Dr. Al Bonikowsky*

From Helga:

Brother Frank, here is the story of my background and how the Lord has led me since I was a two-year-old German girl in Poland.

Some generations back, my German family, the Behnkes, moved to Poland where they could get land very cheaply. There was a lot of land there; and since they were farmers, they decided to immigrate and settle down in that area. When Poland lost the war with Germany, part of the agreement between the countries was that the German people living in Poland had to move to Germany. There was an exchange between the people of the town Zezulin, located in the region of Vartigaw. In 1939, my family who lived in Zezulin was moved to Strohfelde that was closer to Germany. The Polish people that lived in Strohfelde had to move to Zezulin, since we were given their land. No one had a say in the matter. They called it the "German's Farmer Exchange."

I was born in Strohfelde in February 1943. I had two older brothers, and my father was finally drafted into the German military. It was shortly after Dad left that we received word that the Russians were coming to Poland, and we were advised to flee. My mother, with us four children, packed a wagon with the most needful things, hitched two of our best horses, and headed toward Germany. Of course there were a lot of refugees just like us. I don't remember how far we had gone when the Russians caught up with us. Mother said they helped themselves to whatever they wanted. So our horses and wagon were taken along with anything of value. My mother did manage to hide a couple of things.

In January 1944 we finally arrived in Barlinek, northwestern Poland, and stayed there about three months. It was there that the Russians gathered the "older" youth with the promise that they needed them to work for a few hours. They never came back. They took my oldest brother and his friend. They all were crying because they knew what this meant. My parents were godly people, and my mother told me she literally stayed on her knees for three days and nights. On the third day, she heard two pairs of feet running up the stairs. It was my oldest brother and his friend who had run away from their captors.

The first thing the Russians did was shave their heads so that they could easily be identified as having escaped. At dusk the two boys were sent to get water. As soon as they had some cover, they left their buckets and ran. The Russians were not looking for boys that were required to wear an armband that identified them as Polish. My German brother had learned Polish, so he and his friend found the right color fabric and tied it around their arms. They were stopped, but with the right armband color and since they were able to speak Polish perfectly, they were not detained. They ran home across the country and arrived three days later. Our house had an attic, and that is where my brother lived until his hair grew back.

It took us about a year to get to Germany, and my 13-year-old brother Eddy was our food provider. He found an abandoned cow that provided milk. He also found one chicken that laid an egg every day, which was our last meal before we left Barlinek. Since I was just two years old, Eddy always took me in his arms to look for bread, cheese, or anything else. The soldiers and others were always generous when he had me along. I was outgoing, and he said I would go to anyone. From Barlinek we went towards Frankfort An Der Oder, which was the first city in Germany proper. My brother recalls the city being completely deserted with tanks and other war machinery everywhere because the war was over.

There is one story that my mother told me that my oldest brother refused to talk about. Now he says he doesn't remember it, but I have it on tape with mother telling me the story. It must have been in the earlier part of our trip because we still had the horses and wagon, and it was winter. There were a lot of wagons following each other in a snowstorm. We were all stopped because there was no way we could go on through the snow. While there, a man came out of one of the few houses along the road. He came to our wagon and told my mother to take a little road that led away from there and follow it. It would go down into a valley, and there we would find a small community where we would be able to stay for a day or so.

My mother took his advice, and it was just as the man, who my family believed might have been an angel, had said. When we got back onto the main road farther down, we saw what God had spared us from. The Russians had arrived with their big tanks and had literally bulldozed over the line of horses and wagons in their way. We would have been one of them had we not been advised to leave the line. There had been a heavy storm, so things were covered with red snow from the blood of the victims. Why us? Only God knows, but my parents always saw God at work. Mother said that we always had food even if it was just potatoes that we found in a field.

Soon after my father was drafted by the Germans, he was taken prisoner and shipped off to Siberia where he worked in a coal mine. However, soon after his arrival, he became an interpreter between the prisoners and the guards because he could speak Russian. Often under the cover of night, he would go to a nearby town and look up Baptist Christians. They always shared what little they had, and that is what kept him alive. Since Dad was captured early, he never had to use his gun as a soldier, and he was always thankful for that. He was gone for a year; and when he was released, he went back to our home in Poland. Finding that we were gone, he headed toward Germany and found us there. When he found us, we were all sent to a refugee camp because we had nothing.

While we were in the town of Lodingsen in central Germany, we were informed that Argentina would take immigrants. My father wanted to go as far from Communism as possible, so we applied for Argentina. We were informed that Argentina had closed its doors; but Canada had opened theirs, and we could go there—which we did in the spring of 1951. It was handled through the German Baptists and their local church. It was in that German Baptist church that Al and I met. I was only eight and Al was 13, so nothing developed between us until I became a teenager and started dating. Al always says he's glad he didn't have to go to Argentina to find me!

One story that I will never forget is something that happened when we were already in Canada. Our German church had a special speaker visiting from Germany, and we all were there. I didn't know who he was and didn't know if my parents did. When the preacher was speaking, he held everybody's attention when he started to relate a story about a family who had arrived at the refugee camp where he was working. He said that when he asked them about their most pressing needs, they responded that they would like to sing a song of praise to God. Literally translated the song says: "Let your hearts be always joyful and filled with thanksgiving." Then the preacher proceeded to say that the family was in the audience, and would they please stand up. To my great surprise my parents and brothers stood with tears running down their faces. My parents were always very thankful for all God did. I've met people who told me it was my family's testimony that made them come to Christ. My parents lived what they preached! God did so much!

—*Helga Bonikowsky*

VIGNETTE 7

God Knows Your Future

DURING THE thirteen years that I taught at Bob Jones University, one of my responsibilities was to teach Sophomore Music Theory. Theory was one of my main areas of study at the Eastman School of Music. I loved teaching it at BJU, even though it was one of the most difficult undergraduate courses. (I wrote a short version of this lesson in *I, Being in the Way, the Lord Led Me*, but I want to go into more detail here.)

There were five main areas of study in music theory that I believed would help each student become the musician that they needed to be. Although I didn't use this title back then, I used the principle of *God knows your future* to show them how God was working in their lives while they were studying to serve Him later. I believed that every music principle that I taught had a foundation in biblical principles that the students needed to be aware of.

The five "branches" of music theory are: Analysis (understanding how music is constructed); Part Writing (being able to write some music of their own); Sight Singing (being able to read music they have never seen before); Dictation (writing out the music they hear); and Keyboard (being able to play the music on a piano.) I always told the students that they could be glad that I am not a good pianist because it helped me understand what they were going through.

This brings me to one of the most important spiritual lessons that the Lord allowed me to teach every year when I showed up in Sophomore Music Theory at BJU for thirteen years.

The school year was divided into two semesters. At the end of the first semester, I would give the students an exam to see what they were actually learning. After I graded these exams and handed them back to the students (the papers quite often looked like someone had bled all over them from all the red pen marks that I used), I would say to the students: "You know what?! I knew what was on that exam at the beginning of the semester. It was no surprise to me, and I have been trying to get you ready for that exam all during this semester. I think you should have been listening to me."

And then I would say: "You know what?! I already know what is on your final exam that is going to come up at the end of this semester. I am going to try all this semester to get you ready for that exam. Again, I think you ought to listen." And then came the spiritual application: "You know what?! *God knows your future*, and He is trying right now to get you ready for what He knows you will face in the future. It is not going to be a surprise to Him. I think maybe you had better trust Him and not complain about the difficulties you are now facing, but learn the lessons He wants you to learn." I believe more former students have told me that they remember that lesson more than anything I ever taught them about Music Theory.

VIGNETTE 8

"GOD MADE MUSIC" AND "THE HYMNPLAYER"

JOE AND Judy Swaim have been our good friends since they were our students in the early 1960's. They both studied music theory with me. Joe was my trombone student, and Judy studied hymn playing with Flora Jean. These two dedicated Christian musicians have had an effective ministry for almost half a century through the many quality products they have produced for their company, Praise Hymn Inc., a Christian music education curricula. They both graduated from BJU, Judy in 1965 and Joe in 1966.

Flora Jean and I feel privileged to have had a small part in Joe and Judy's lives. They have been an immense blessing to us.

As I am writing this, Joe has renal cancer. His experience with his sickness is like what C. S. Lewis calls the "law of undulation" or what Winston Churchill experienced in his up-and-down life as "the rolling English road." Joe and Judy have demonstrated that: "Blessed is the man . . . who passing through the valley of Baca (weeping), make it a well." Psalm 84:5-6.

I want to let Judy explain how the "law of undulation" has affected them and how they have responded to it over the years.

My class was '63; however, I had not done my student teaching. Walt Fremont let me do it in my minor at the Academy after we got married. Joe completed a year at the University of Miami in Coral Gables while we taught at Dade Christian School in Miami for two years then returned to BJU for Joe to complete his senior year.

Presently, Joe has renal cancer. One kidney was removed in '04. He was diagnosed with cancer a week after Claire, our granddaughter, was born. The Lord was kind to let us enjoy that birth before the bad news. The doctors thought the kidney contained the cancer and that would be the end of it; however, it came back in his thyroid. Removing the thyroid would take care of the problem; however, while running scans, the doctor found tumors on his adrenal gland and pancreas. They gave him 24-36 months to live. He took chemo in a pill form for two years. By that time he was suffering from side effects. In January of this year, the doctor recommended another type of chemo that would give him six months; however, without any chemo, he would still only have six months, so Joe decided to stop the chemo. He has a better quality of life once he quit taking poison. We have been blessed to have these three years to prepare.

—Judy Johnson Swaim

Knowing this, I am glad I asked Joe to write something for this book because he and Judy have been doing what I believe should be the purpose of any Christian. Here is Joe Swaim's testimony:

It was a typical trombone lesson during the last half of my senior year at Bob Jones University. At the end of the lesson, Dr. Garlock asked me what plans Judy and I had after graduation. I said we had a few possibilities but that we had not made any decisions. Dr. Garlock mentioned that he knew of a school in Pensacola, Florida that had openings for a band director and piano teacher. He offered to contact Dr. and Mrs. Horton at Pensacola Christian School and arrange an interview if we were interested. So on a rainy weekend in the spring, Judy and I drove to Pensacola and met with the Hortons. We quickly decided that Pensacola was the place where the Lord wanted us to be.

While teaching at Pensacola we found it difficult to find material for their elementary music class instruction. Years later, while living in Texas, I mentioned to Judy that I wanted to start a publishing company, and I wanted us to write a complete music education curricula for use in Christian schools. In 1973, with no money and no experience in business, we started Praise Hymn, Inc. We began working on our project which we called "God Made Music," and within a year we had grades 1 through 6 completed, printed, and selling briskly.

That may have been one of the most valuable trombone lessons ever. Not for what I learned that day on the trombone, but because of Frank Garlock's interest in our future. It was during those years in Pensacola that we were made aware of the need for Christian music education curricula. Years after leaving Pensacola, the Lord brought that need to our attention again. At the writing of this book, "God Made Music" is approaching 45 years in publication. Thanks be to our Lord for this opportunity, and thanks to Dr. Garlock for his interest in seeing that his students continue in the Lord.

In 1975 Judy and Flora Jean Garlock led a joint seminar on hymn arranging at the Christian Education Association convention in Tampa, Florida. Many of those who attended encouraged them to put their ideas in print so others could learn how to arrange hymns. Judy and Flora Jean called their new hymn playing series—"The Hymnplayer." Judy wrote her part in Texas, and Flora Jean wrote hers in South Carolina. In 1976, everyone met at Horticultural Printers in Mesquite, Texas to watch the books roll off the press. Since 1976, "The Hymnplayer" has been used by many church pianists, teachers, and students to develop their hymn playing ability for the Lord. The original 12-volume "Hymnplayer" has been newly revised to four books with additional downloads online.

When Judy first attended Bob Jones University, composing your "own" piano arrangement was something few attempted. It was Flora Jean who encouraged and taught hymn playing and arranging to her many piano students. Judy and I appreciate her impact on hymn playing and count it a privilege for Praise Hymn, Inc. to be a part of her ongoing teaching ministry.

—*Harry Joe Swaim*

VIGNETTE 9

THE NEW YORK PHILHARMONIC

THIS MAY seem like an unusual vignette to include in this book, but I believe it shows how God works when we decide to do His will and in the process give up something we would really like to do. From the time I was a small boy and started to play the trombone, I wanted one day to be a "great trombonist." I worked hard at it and had some good teachers.

At age thirteen, I had learned to read all the different clefs that a trombonist might have to know. Someone had given me the Vladislav Blazevich Clef Studies that contains strenuous clef studies in which there were clef changes right in the middle of sixteenth-note runs. In addition to the bass clef, there were the tenor and the alto clef exercises. For some strange reason, I loved working on these exercises; and my ability to play all the clefs got me into the New Jersey All-State High School Orchestra when I was 13.

That opened the door for me to play during my teenage years in a number of small orchestras in northern New Jersey, including the very small Mountain Lakes Symphony Orchestra. It just so happened that there were several players in that particular orchestra who also played in the New York Philharmonic at that time, 1948. When they heard me playing the cello part, sometimes in tenor clef (when the main cellist could not be there) or the viola part that is in alto clef, they were amazed and arranged for me to sit in with the New York Philharmonic. These outstanding musicians, including the Mountain Lakes orchestra conductor, even made contacts for me with the Julliard School of Music in New York to study there on a scholarship. The idea was that someday I could be the principal trombonist in the New York Philharmonic.

You can imagine their surprise, when in January 1949, I announced to these musicians that I was going to Bob Jones University to study. One of them admonished me very strongly by saying: "You don't realize what an opportunity we are giving you! Why in the world would you ever give up the New York Philharmonic to go to a little redneck school like Bob Jones? You will be sorry someday!"

Well, let me say right here that I have never been sorry!! God, by His grace, took me to BJU where I could not only learn how to serve Him, but to find my wife to whom I have been married for 65 years.

But as Paul Harvey would say: "That is not the rest of the story!" In 1962, after I had been teaching at BJU for only two years, God impressed Don Harwood's parents to send him to BJU to study music and to study trombone with me. Don was already a good bass trombonist when he came to BJU, and I must admit that I did not know much about the bass trombone at that point. I had never played a bass trombone, and I was not very familiar with the orchestra literature that included a bass trombone. In fact, I always conveyed to my students, including Don Harwood, that my purpose in being at BJU and teaching there was not to train them to be professional orchestra players, but to prepare them to use their talents in service for the Lord. However, I had studied with Emory Remington at the Eastman School of Music as well as with other great teachers, including Enrico Bozacco of the Metropolitan Opera orchestra. Because I came directly from my studies at the Eastman School of Music, I was able to impart to Don and my other students—some of what I had learned from "The Chief," as Remington is still known as to this day. When I studied with him, this masterful teacher had one of his former students in every major orchestra in the United States.

Don Harwood was the only trombone student in my 13 years of teaching at BJU that was allowed to major in Trombone Performance. Don played in many of the brass ensembles, including the Trombone Choir. In his last year of study, he played *Allegro et Finale* by Eugene Bozza, a difficult trombone concerto performed at the BJU Commencement Concert. He then went from BJU to the West Point Military Academy Band in 1966, then to the Metropolitan Opera Orchestra in 1969, and finally to the New York Philharmonic Orchestra in 1975. He kept that Bass Trombone position, of which there is only one, for 32 years.

Why this story? I never got to be the principal trombonist of that great orchestra. However, although I don't think Don ever realized it, through Don I vicariously showed up and became a part of the New York Philharmonic.

I had a younger brother, David, who followed me by eleven years with an opportunity to attend the Julliard School of Music in New York. His musical ability was piano performance. His choice was to pursue that area and become a professional concert pianist. He even studied with Madame Rosina Lhevinne at Julliard, and she was "regarded as one of the great pianist master/teachers of all time."

However, the prevailing atmosphere, environment and influence of the New York City artistic community that seems to capture many of those who become a part of it, captured David and led him to a tragic death at age 27. My mother told me that David told her not long before he died: "If an evangelist would have me, I would love to go with him as his pianist." Unfortunately, that desire was never realized. God protected me from an ungodly lifestyle, even when I did not realize He was doing it. I will be eternally grateful that He did.

Again, "That is not the rest of the story!" On November 10, 2015, Dan Turner and Paul Jantz, two of my former students who are now on the music faculty at BJU, decided to do something special for their former teacher. They contacted many former trombone players who at one time or another had been in the Trombone Choir at BJU, during its 55-year history, to come to the university to be a part of an artist series called "Trombonanza." The concert featured the BJU Symphonic Wind Band and many of my former trombone students under the direction of Dr. Dan Turner. Also, Matthew Vaughn was the featured guest artist.

Dr. Dan Turner has been the director of bands at BJU for thirty-three years. Paul Jantz has been the director of the BJU Trombone Choir for the past thirty-five years.

The guest artist, Matthew Vaughn (who holds the distinguished co-principal trombone position of the Philadelphia Orchestra), is the finest trombonist that I have ever heard. However, the surprising part of the story is that they wanted to honor me and were able to bring 56 trombone players to play together as a trombone choir that evening under the direction of Matthew Vaughn.

These musicians came from 19 states and one foreign country to be a part of this unique celebration. Some were my former students, (one from 1960), some were my students' students, and others were *their* current students. As far as I am able to find out, there has never been a trombone choir that large, anywhere in the world. I googled "trombone choirs," and the largest one I could find was about thirty-seven players at Luther College.

Here are some quotes from the program:

> "Frank Garlock will always be 'Dr. G.' to us, his former students... His energy was boundless; he taught us with passion and humor. He shared Christ with us in class, in lessons, in rehearsals, and on the sidewalks. He demanded our best, and we frankly thought he knew just about everything—his intellectual curiosity was astounding (and still is)—he is a trombone/euphonium pedagogue, music theorist, arranger, composer, conductor, church musician, author, athlete, pilot, and preacher . . .

> Frank studied trombone with arguably America's greatest teacher, Emory Remington, and played in the Eastman Trombone Choir. He imported this medium to South Carolina (and perhaps even the Southeast!) when he began teaching at BJU in 1960.

> BJU's trombone choir gained national recognition in 1965 when the group performed at the national Music Educators conference in a one-hour program of [brass] music—all memorized! Little did the audience know that everything performed on the BJU campus in those days was memorized!"

This honor from my former students at BJU was much greater to me than anything I ever could have received from being a part of the New York Philharmonic Orchestra. All I could think of as I was relishing the privilege to play my trombone with the other fifty-five trombonists (including my son, Randy, and my grandson, Jason) that evening was: I just showed up! and God did it all!

VIGNETTE 10

REFLECTING GOD'S CHARACTER

I KNEW George Mackey when he was a student at BJU in 1963. George always had a good sense of humor, although it was sometimes more humor than sense. He was always well known and liked as a student. It was also obvious then that he wanted to serve the Lord and be used by Him. Flora Jean and I have been with George and Carol Mackey in several places where they have served the Lord. We have always appreciated their faithfulness and desire for the Lord to use them wherever He took them.

In 2013, the Mackeys moved to Greenville and began attending Faith Baptist Church where we attend. George has always played a baritone horn, and we sat next to each other as he began to play his instrument in the orchestra at our church.

One day at church, a beautiful lady came to me to tell me what a blessing my teaching had been to her husband over the years of their ministry. Unfortunately, I did not recognize her; and when I saw George, I told him what the lady had said. You can imagine my surprise and embarrassment when he told me that nice lady was his wife, Carol. That's when I asked the Mackeys to write out a little of what Carol said to me.

These are several of the biblical principles we learned and applied to our lives personally and throughout the forty-five years of ministry, some in the pastorate, some as assistant in youth and music, and some in ministry to Christian schools.

The first thing you presented to those of us in the music ministry was your book *The Big Beat: A Rock Blast*, (first printed in 1970). That book gave us biblical reasons for having the right kind of music. Then as you presented your seminars called "The Symphony of Life," you directed us to the Scriptural basis for music in a believer's life in Psalm 96:1, "Oh sing to the LORD a new song." We were impressed with the fact that our music is to be different!—different from before salvation; different from the music of the world.

George and I both attended public school, so we knew well the music that the unsaved listened to. He was unsaved during his teen years, and I worked at a popular restaurant where multitudes of quarters were deposited in the jukebox. My Dad sang in a nightclub before he was saved; and as a very young child, I was aware of the change that took place in the music, both the style and the words he sang.

The principle of separation was clearly taught, and we both understood it. George knew changes in his life were needed right after he was saved at nineteen. I came to know the Lord as a seven-year-old, so understood throughout my years that if I reflected Jesus Christ in my life, I would think, act, speak, and dress differently than other young people. You used to give the diagram of two intersecting circles and a line of demarcation representing "the world." As the world changed position on things, Christians would remain the same distance from "the world," but as the circles grew farther and farther from the standard of the Word of God, so would both circles move farther and farther away. So in time, Christians stayed the same distance from the world but became farther and farther from the standard of the Word of God. The philosophy changed. You emphasized that music was to be God-centered, and it became man-centered as time went by, appealing first to the flesh, then to the spirit.

You explained how to compare music to the right standards of good music. Our music was to reflect the character of God. You helped us understand and evaluate music with sensual qualities. You stressed the fact that biblical music reached the physical part of man, but that was the last effect. God's kind of music goes from the spiritual to the physical, not the physical first. You taught us that there are absolutes in good music. You gave us examples, made explanations, and used the quotes of the writers of the world's music to help us understand their purposes and philosophies. Our purpose is to glorify God in all we do and elevate God. Their purpose is not ours; the very basis of their philosophy is not God-centered but man-centered. You helped us evaluate music in its entirety, not just the words. You helped us understand the meaning of discernment in the area of music.

Our Eternal Standard, the perfect Word of God, has not changed; and we praise the Lord that your position has not changed, Dr. Garlock. We love you and thank the Lord for your influence in our lives.

—George and Carol Mackey

We lost our tuba player in our church orchestra last year because he "graduated" to a new ministry in serving the Lord. George, still wanting to serve the Lord, immediately picked up that instrument and began working on playing it. He is doing a great job. In fact, this last Sunday (August 10, 2015) he played the tuba in our church's brass ensemble. The ensemble played one of my difficult arrangements that I originally wrote for brass students at the Eastman School of Music. George played the tuba part well!

I should also mention that the Lord is still using Carol to speak to ladies' seminars. Her vast experience as the wife of a pastor, as the wife of a youth and music minister, and finally in Christian schools (all being married to the same man) gives her a broad outlook of all that is involved in these varied capacities. Many ladies are learning from the wisdom that the Lord has given this dedicated wife and faithful servant of God.

VIGNETTE 11

ABRAHAM'S SERVANT

I HAVE been fascinated by the story in Genesis 24 for a long time. This is the account of Abraham sending his servant to Mesopotamia to get a bride for his son Isaac. Every time I read this vignette in the Bible, I am amazed at how God worked in both Abraham and in his servant's life to accomplish His purpose. In fact, for many years when I was asked to speak at Christian education conferences, I would use this story. I titled it "How to Be Happy with Your Boss" in order to encourage teachers in Christian schools to have a good relationship with the board and principal of the school in which they taught. I believe I was probably asked to do this because of my experience as a principal of a Christian school in Pensacola, Florida from 1954 to 1957.

The Wilds is a Christian camp and conference center in Rosman, North Carolina. I had the wonderful opportunity to be the music director when the camp opened with one hundred fifty teenagers for just three weeks on August 4, 1969. What God has accomplished through the ministry of The Wilds over the last 46 years is almost unbelievable. Over half a million young people have attended summer camp with an average of seven hundred fifty campers each week. The Wilds also holds camps for men, ladies, juniors, families, businessmen, and preachers, (to mention just a few of the programs the camp hosts regularly). In addition to that, the staff of The Wilds are privileged to disciple two hundred fifty eager Christian counselors and about twelve hundred sponsors who come to camp with their teens for almost three months every year.

Ken Hay, one of the founders and the first director of The Wilds, asked me to give my message on Genesis 24 at one of the banquets that was being held to raise interest and support for this new camp. Ken Collier, who later became the Camp Director and then the President of The Wilds, heard me give that message at that banquet. Here is his testimony concerning how the Lord used that message when I just showed up about 45 years ago:

God began to arrest my attention in my junior and senior years of high school. Until then, I had spent life riding the fence spiritually with emphasis on popularity in my public school. As the Lord does with proud people, He was resisting my way continually. Somehow, I ran across the very old book, *In His Steps*, by Charles M. Sheldon; and I was curious about the subtitle, "What would Jesus do?" For me to read anything but required reading was a wondrous thing in itself, but I actually did keep it by my bed and pick it up from time to time. Although I thought the book was archaic and behind the times, the question hung in my mind—"What would Jesus do? At this same time, my Bible reading centered on Philippians 2, the great "emptying" of Christ when He came down to earth. Having read and heard many things about Christ, I had to try to put together in my mind the question of how did it make sense that Christ was the King, yet He became a servant and humbled Himself and died on the cross?

I began to practice the question, "What would Jesus do?" in some of the arenas of my life. Of course, the question not anchored in the Bible is dangerous. I'm sure sometimes I would answer what He would do with my thoughts rather than His words. However, it stirred something deeply in my soul. In September 1968, having graduated in May of the same year, I enrolled at Bob Jones University and was reunited with one of my mentors, Ken Hay, my former camp director in my area camp. Ken Hay had taught me the importance of having a daily time with God, a "God & I" time. Seeing him around the campus made me read God's Word more faithfully. This was about the year Ken Hay was recruiting help for this brand new, start-up camp called The Wilds. Camp meant a great deal to me. So I signed up to go that pioneer year, much to the chagrin of my mother and my girlfriend back home.

After an amazing inaugural summer camp in 1969, I was hooked on The Wilds. The Wilds was sponsoring a fund-raising banquet in the fall of 1969 or 1970 in the Greenville, SC area. It was a time of rejoicing and sharing how God was graciously changing the lives of many young people through the camp ministry. There was a good spirit at that banquet. I cannot remember if I had a part in the program or was just there because of my wholesale affection for the ministry of the camp or for free food (college guy). Frank Garlock, my "music director" that first summer, gave a challenge from God's Word that evening about Abraham's servant from Genesis 24. It would change my life.

From the introduction, I was transfixed. He talked about "Abraham's servant who ruled over all he had." "How can a servant rule over anything?" I puzzled. The more he got into the passage, the more it astounded me that this was actually a pattern of Christ's leadership in Philippians 2. The servant had authority, but he used it to serve! The servant prayed specifically for blessing on His master's mission. The servant was filled with anticipation of God bringing success to the venture. He would not quit until he had finished his mission. He expressed gratefulness for the privilege of being used as a servant. The clincher for me was when the servant mentioned that as he was "in the way" the Lord used him. As the greatest servant Who ever lived, Christ while going along the way His Father mapped for Him, changed all of our lives with His love, obedience, humility, and sacrifice as a servant. Abraham's servant, who ruled over all he had, was just a little peek at how we can be excited servants to the Great Servant. I thank the Lord for Frank Garlock "getting in the way" that evening some 45 years ago and being led of God to teach the lesson of the "servant, who ruled." I learned something about my King, Who rules and yet serves, and it changed my life and ministry.

—Ken Collier

VIGNETTE 12

FORTY-THREE YEARS LATER

I HAVE had the privilege to be on the board of the WILDS Christian Camp since it was founded in 1969. I was the first music director of the camp until Ron Hamilton took over for me. I have spoken at the camp many times since then. I attend the board meetings whenever I can and am always thrilled to see what the Lord has done through that international ministry in reaching, challenging, and training young people to serve the Lord.

Gordon Dickson was the venerated youth pastor from 1984 to 1994 of the Faith Baptist Church where Flora Jean and I presently attend. Church members give glowing reports of the ministry he has had among the young people of our church. He also has been the pastor of the outstanding Calvary Baptist Church in Findlay, Ohio, where he has ministered for 22 years.

It was at The Wilds board meeting in November 2015 that Pastor Dickson, who is also on the board, pulled me aside and said that there was something he would like to tell me. Here is Brother Dickson's account of what had happened 43 years before:

> In 1972, I attended the December "holiday retreat" at *The Wilds Christian Camp and Conference Center* in Rosman, North Carolina. Dr. Garlock was one of the speakers at this retreat. One morning, he gave a challenge on the topic of Biblical meditation. For all eternity, I will thank the Lord for the effect that this message had upon me.

One year earlier, on December 29, 1971, I had trusted Christ under the faithful, biblical preaching of Coach "Rock" Royer and Dr. Ken Hay. When I returned to my home in Pensacola, Florida, I was rejoicing in my new life in Christ. Though I attended a Christian school, my family also attended a liberal church that had lost its biblical moorings. So my first year as a believer was somewhat chaotic. I read my Bible occasionally but had no genuine assurance of eternal life. As a result of the false doctrinal teaching of my church, I assumed that I had lost my salvation and regained it repeatedly. You can well imagine how "double-minded" I felt: full of doubts and fears.

Then the Lord greatly blessed me through the message on biblical meditation given by Frank Garlock. I have no doubt that God's grace labored mightily in him that day, and it made a powerful impact on me. I was thrilled to be back in the place where the Spirit of God had moved me so deeply. I listened to the beginning of the message with interest; I walked away from his message gripped with the necessity of meditating in the Scriptures. It is essential to "let the word of Christ dwell in you richly" (Colossians 3:16). At the end of his message, Dr. Garlock gave a simple, practical invitation as we bowed to pray. He asked for a show of hands for all those who would make a simple decision; who among us would tell the Lord that we would read and think through one vignette of Proverbs each day for the next 31 days? I slipped my hand up, and apparently another young man did as well. Brother Garlock said, "There are two young men who have raised their hands. I believe that the Lord will greatly bless their lives as you carry through on this decision."

I don't know anything about the other guy, but I can testify that putting Brother Garlock's message into practice transformed my life. Within the next month, all my doubts about my salvation were swept away. I continued to read Proverbs and went on to feast in the Gospels and Psalms. God radically changed my thinking and gave me a bold new confidence. Within a few months, the Lord had given this shy, backward boy an earnest desire to preach the Word. The Lord had done so much for me through His Word that I wanted to share His blessings with others.

Even now, a regular feature of my preaching includes the questions: "Are you getting that 'one thought' every day out of God's Word? Are you meditating in the Scriptures?" The fountain of blessing that broke forth on that cold December day at The Wilds continues to overflow into the lives of others to this very day. To God be the glory!"

—Pastor Gordon Dickson

VIGNETTE 13

BIBLICAL MEDITATION

IN 1954, the Lord led me to the Brent Baptist Church in Pensacola, Florida to be the Minister of Music, the Youth Pastor, and the Education Director. After being there for a little over a year, the Lord also led me to be the Principal of Brent Christian School. This was exactly one year after Arlin and Beka Horton began Pensacola Christian School. They were a tremendous help to this novice to do things for which I had had no training. The story of how the Lord helped me at that time is in my book *I, Being in the Way, the Lord Led Me.*

My experiences there have placed me in positions to counsel many young people throughout my years serving the Lord. Much of my ministry has been with teens: at Pensacola, Rochester, Youth for Christ, and with the Wilds. While teaching at BJU, I taught a married-couples Sunday school class of over 500 people. Teaching this class gave me the opportunity to counsel young couples, many of whom were students at BJU. That our sovereign God is in control, and that we need to trust Him completely was at the center of my counseling.

One of the tools that has helped me personally is the Biblical principle of meditation that is so clearly taught in the Word of God. (Joshua 1:8; Psalm 1:2; Psalm 23:2; and Psalm 104:34, the verse that comes right after my "life verse.") The devil has many counterfeits of the meditation principle, but they do not invalidate the real thing.

I developed a four-point outline (the original probably came from someone else) that God has used to help people. Gordon Dickson, who is the subject of the vignette called "Forty-Three Years Later" [Vignette 12] is just an example of one who took the principle to heart and saw it change his life.

The four-point outline is based on Psalm 19:7 —"The law of the LORD is perfect (complete or sufficient) <u>converting the soul</u>." The law never saves anybody (Galatians 3:24), but it is "a schoolmaster" to bring us to Christ. The "soul" is made up of (1) the mind, (2) the will, and (3) the emotions. I have added a fourth aspect to these three because (4) the heart must also be involved (Psalm 19:14.) The four principles need to be "converted" by biblical meditation as the rest of Psalm 19 makes clear:

THE MIND —by **Memorizing** Scripture that applies to your
    situation (Find Scripture about the problem you are facing. Apply
    the "medicine" where it is needed.)

THE WILL —by **Visualizing** the application of the Scripture to the
    situation (Joseph's dreams were visualizations of the will of God.
    The parables of Jesus are visualizations of spiritual truth.)

THE EMOTIONS —by **Personalizing** the Scripture to yourself
    (Isaiah 26:3—"Thou wilt keep **ME** in perfect peace, [because] **MY**
    MIND is stayed on Thee.")

THE HEART —by **Utilizing** the Scripture in real life
    (Mathew 7:24-27 —The wise man "**doeth them**" The foolish man
    "**doeth them not**." Psalm 119 —The idea of keeping or doing is
    there about 30 times, and meditation is there six times.)

Success and prosperity are <u>always</u> tied to meditation in the Scripture.

Psalm 1:2-3 —"His delight is in the law of the Lord; and in His law doth he **meditate** day and night. And he shall be like a tree planted by the rivers of water, that bringeth forth his fruit in his season; his leaf also shall not wither; and **whatsoever he doeth shall prosper.**"

Joshua 1:8 —"This book of the law shall not depart out of thy mouth; but thou shalt **meditate** therein day and night, that thou mayest observe to do according to all that is written therein; for then thou shalt make thy way **prosperous**, and then thou shalt have good **success.**"

Deuteronomy 29:9 —"Keep (carefully follow or **meditate** on) therefore the words of this covenant, and do them, [utilize them by doing them with your heart,] that ye may **prosper** in all that ye do."

I Timothy 4:15 —"**Meditate** upon these things; give thyself wholly to them; that thy **profitting** may appear to all."

One Scripture that most people miss is in Psalm 23:1-2 —"The LORD is my shepherd; I shall not want. He maketh me to **lie down** in green pastures." (Sheep eat when they are standing up. When they "lie down," they are doing what cows do. They eat the food and then lie down to "chew the cud." They are "ruminants" that bring it back up to chew on it or revolve it and masticate it.) This is how the Psalmist, who knows sheep, calls himself one of the Lord's sheep, and says that he "lies down" in green pastures to digest (**meditate**) on what his Shepherd has fed him from His Word.

If you want to have the kind of success and prosperity that God promises, try practicing the principle of mediation that *activates* the Word of God in your heart. I suggest that you particularly meditate on the book of Proverbs, as Gordon Dickson did, and let the Lord change your life.

VIGNETTE 14

A PROFOUND IMPACT

G OD BROUGHT the Garlocks and the Woetzels together in an unusual way, but in His timing. If you have my autobiography, *I, Being in the Way*, you will find on page 101 that our meeting was at the Northeastern Bible College in Essex Fells, New Jersey. This is where the representative from the college who picked me up at the airport said: "I think you need to know that the faculty does not want you here." It became obvious very quickly that the students did not want me there either.

As a result of the meeting in Essex Fells, the Lord led Kurt and Suzanne Woetzel in a marvelous way to have a ministry for more than 35 years. Their ministry has not been confined to New Hampshire but has extended throughout the New England states and beyond. I have asked the Woetzels to write their story for this book. It demonstrates what God does when we just show up to follow His will.

No man has had a more profound impact on our service for the Lord in music ministry than Frank Garlock.

In 1953, the Lord brought the Woetzel family out from behind the Iron Curtain of East Germany in a miraculous way. I was nine years old. With a few suitcases in hand, we left comfort, stability, home, business, relatives, and dear Christian friends. There was much risk involved. Had our plans and actions been discovered, our family would have been dissolved and none of us would ever have seen the

light of day again. The Lord graciously provided safe passage to West Berlin and ultimately to a much-cherished
land of freedom in the United States. We are reminded
daily of His wonderful leading and providential care.

Little did we know that just a few miles from our new
home in New Jersey, the Lord was preparing a man. This
man would later become an encourager, an example, and
a catalyst for my wife, Suzanne, and me to be involved in
service to the Savior in local-church music ministry.

In the late 1970's we found ourselves in a church which was
beginning to vacillate in its ministry philosophy. Among
other concerns, the vacillating included experimenting
with music which, we were convinced, was inappropriate
for the believer both at church and at home. We were
intrinsically involved in music ministry at that church.
While trying to find answers for our new dilemma, a friend
suggested that we listen to the *Symphony of Life Seminar*
cassettes by Dr. Frank Garlock.

When these arrived in our home, we listened intently
and quickly discovered that there was someone, rather
eloquent and knowledgeable, who had the same objec-
tion to the new sound as we. His biblical approach, logical
presentation, and obviously well-prepared information
caused us to investigate more. After numerous phone
calls, we discovered that he was to speak at a Christian
college in New Jersey. And "it just so happened" that I had
a business meeting close to that college during the days
that he was to speak. Yes, for us it was the first instance
where God's leading in our lives was apparent.

We attended one of his meetings at the college. He was under severe fire. The students openly challenged him and mocked his presentation with laughter and rude verbal interruptions. It became obvious that he was brought in by the administration to deal with an issue which they could not handle. Frank stood his ground graciously. He continued to present Scripture as well as secular data to make his case.

This experience showed us, in a very dramatic manner, the intensity of the coming battle over music. The battle had not yet reached the churches. But it would. The "sides" were just beginning to gather on the campuses. It would be a matter of a few short years when those who were at this college and others "preparing for ministry" would become the new leaders in the churches. The die was cast. Now, in hindsight, we were witnessing the beginning of a growing tsunami. The man who was spending his resources, energy, focus, and life holding his hand in the crumbling dyke was Frank Garlock. Clearly another instance of God's direction for us was developing.

In our initial research, we also discovered he would soon be speaking in Gorham, New Hampshire. Living in Contoocook, we decided that this was another perfect opportunity to hear him, talk with him, and yes, encourage him. We had gained an interest in his ministry by watching him under attack. His music philosophy was our philosophy. His burden became our burden. Even though it was a bit premature, we felt the Lord knitting our hearts together in an unusual way. Suzanne and I met him for dinner in Gorham.

A few months later, on another business trip, we found ourselves in Greenville, SC attending the church where Frank served as music director. He returned the Gorham-dinner favor by inviting us for lunch after the service. We met his wife Flora Jean. Little did we know that a long-term friendship and a joyous serving the Lord together would ensue.

In 1978 Frank came to speak at our church in Concord. We were still in that church actively serving as music volunteers. The Garlock meetings lasted Wednesday through Friday evening. The attendance was high. Frank preached boldly, compassionately, and specifically about the ills of the new music's influence in the churches collectively and in homes of families individually. On the last night of the meetings, over forty people came forward to make decisions. I was a deacon at that church. At the next meeting of the deacons, the comment was made, "Of course we can't have Frank Garlock back again. His preaching was much too strong." The majority of deacons agreed. We knew it was time for us to consider another ministry. In essence, Frank Garlock would in part be responsible for what was to follow in Concord.

Hundreds of miles from Concord, in God's perfect timing, the Lord tugged at the heart of a pastor to move to New Hampshire and plant a new church in our city. Believers had been praying. In 1980 that church began in our living room with its founding pastor. Over the years, it grew exponentially. What started with thirteen in attendance at the first service grew to over 900. The Christian school of that ministry caused young people to prepare themselves for full-time Christian service. Many of them are still serving

Him faithfully today. The Lord also drew many good musicians to that church. The choir blossomed to about 85. The church became the "flagship" in the New England area. It annually hosted a one-day conference which would draw over 900 believers from the outside eager to sing and praise the Lord. They were taught and encouraged in how to more effectively serve the Lord in their ministry.

As the church grew, Suzanne and I sensed the need to get formal music training. Where should we go to get that training? Being in business full-time would not allow really long stretches of education. As the Lord would have it, Frank Garlock began a Masters of Sacred Music graduate program. This program was designed for those who desired training in voice, conducting, and piano. The program was three weeks for four summers leading to a degree. It fit us perfectly. Suzanne did her work in voice and I in conducting. Yes, for us it was another instance where we just needed to show up.

The Garlocks and we had become quite good friends; but attending this program would bring our friendship to a whole new level. When we arrived for our first three-week session, Frank picked us up at the airport. We were thrilled. I will never forget his words when he deposited us at the administration building. He said, "Kurt, we're good friends. But now I'll also become your teacher. I hope we can make that work well." I became a little choked up and said, "I'm certain we can make that work." And work well it did.

The teachers were Frank Garlock (conducting, music theory, hymnology), Flora Jean (piano), and Ray and Ann Gibbs (voice). The program was ideally suited. It was perfect for the volunteer church musicians like us. It addressed the needs of those serving part-time in music ministry while also working full-time secular jobs. It also was extremely helpful for full-time church music directors. The academic demands were high. But it was fun. The work load was intense, both during the three summer weeks and the months between. We were stretched because we had a master teacher who was accustomed to being stretched and expected the same from his students. Under Frank's leadership, the student body enjoyed the four summers so much that the seniors were disappointed when gradu-ation finally arrived. We had become a family. We had a great team of teachers dedicated to serving the Lord.

The whole experience prepared us well for the growth which was taking place at our church in Concord. I left the business world and was appointed as music director of the church which began in our living room. Who influenced that move and caused a passion to become an avocation? Our now even closer friend, Frank Garlock.

Much has happened since graduating from that program. Frank asked Suzanne and me to join Majesty's MusiCollege. This is a team of about a dozen musicians who travel to several churches each summer doing two-day conferences with various music workshops. The two days end with a delegate choir and faculty concert. We served with that effort for twelve years. It was wonderful.

Shortly after graduating from the graduate program, Frank and I jointly authored *Music in the Balance*. This book achieved respectable circulation and gained considerable music-thinking influence in our circle of churches. Since its release, it has been expanded to a thirteen-class series ready to be taught in a school setting with well over 400 PowerPoint® slides in addition to the fifty-six recorded music examples illustrating the concepts in the text.

What is now most rewarding, encouraging, and soul-stirring is being able to point to, and often hear from, young people who are Christian school teachers, song leaders, Sunday school teachers, choir directors, missionaries, and even pastors that participated in our music groups. We had an opportunity to mold their thinking in classes, chapel hours, school and church choirs, one-on-one music instruction, and through everyday personal interactions. Our hearts are overjoyed and our eyes get moist when we now attend a conference, visit a church or school and discover those who have remained faithful in philosophy, practice, and direction due to the efforts made during their formative years. In the final analysis, these are truly Garlock "grandchildren" serving the Lord as a direct result of the training we received.

The opening sentence, "No man has had a more profound impact on our service for the Lord in music ministry than Frank Garlock," is not an exaggeration. It may well be an understatement. The ramifications of all that took place as a result of one man's faithfulness will not be known until we enter heaven.

With much love and grateful hearts,

—Kurt & Suzanne Woetzel - Psalm 69:30

VIGNETTE 15

THE AIERDI MIRACLE

IN 1985, Flora Jean and I were thanking the Lord for all the opportunities we were having to serve Him. We rejoiced in the growth of the ministry of Majesty Music.

When we first established Majesty Music, we said that we would always take part of the income we received and reinvest it in the Lord's work in another place, particularly in missions. The Sunday school class I taught was giving to many mission projects, and we wanted to do something personally as well.

Andy Bonikowsky and Mimi Allen had just married the same year. Flora Jean and I sang at their wedding. We had known them both since they were young children, and we wanted to invest in them and their future ministry. Andy's parents (Al and Helga) were missionaries in the Basque region of northern Spain [Vignette 6] and Mimi's parents (Flay and Margaret) were missionaries in the Southeast region of that same country [Vignette 3]. All four of these missionaries had been in the Sunday school class that I taught, and we had taken an interest in their ministries as we had a special relationship with each of them.

We knew that Andy and Mimi, having grown up helping their parents on the mission field, had probably not had many new clothes. Therefore, we came up with the idea of taking this young married couple to downtown Greenville and buying them some new clothes. When we arrived at the store, we were surprised to learn that neither one of them knew what size they wore because they had only hand-me-downs all their lives. What a privilege it was to just show up and be able to buy this young missionary couple the first new clothes they ever had.

When we visited Andy and Mimi Bonikowsky in Beasain after they had been ministering there for thirteen years, they had only 13 people attending their church. This was not because, as missionaries, they did not know the language. Since Andy and Mimi grew up in Spain, they both spoke excellent Spanish.

The Bonikowskys were very diligent in passing out thousands of tracts and canvassing all the surrounding villages where they live in Spain with few "results." The customs and mindset of the people made it very difficult to win them to Christ. If a person lets anyone know he has trusted Christ, he will be ostracized by his family, probably lose his job, and be rejected by everyone he knows.

However, through a special series of events, God led the Bonikowskys to buy an old farmhouse (about 300 years old) in the mountains. They fixed it up with the help of Andy's father and used it for the Lord in many ways. The miracles the Lord used to enable the Bonikowskys to obtain this property are written in a book called *The Aierdi Miracle*. This book tells the story of how God's challenge to Abraham to "count the stars" came to life in an unusual way (Genesis 15:5).

God amazingly worked in this ministry in Aierdi. The Lord led them to hold camp conferences for children of missionaries from all over Europe. One result of starting this camp is that their church is now having over 70 attend to their church services. Through Aierdi, they are reaping results and having a tremendous influence for the Lord in an extremely difficult area to serve Him. Andy tells his version of their incredible story.

Both Mimi's family and mine have known Dr. and Mrs. Garlock since the two of us were kids. In the 1970s his Sunday school class lessons, taught at our home church, were often the subject of our family conversations. Why, not even on the foreign mission field could we escape his influence! The weekly cassette tapes made their way over the ocean and into our Spanish apartments, bringing spiritual blessing and challenge to us in our own language.

One of my more memorable moments with the Garlocks came as I returned to the United States for college in 1985. They handed me my first ever experience of being measured for a suit! Those gray pants and navy sport coat were my treasure for years, not only because of their high quality, but also because they came from someone so important to us. In fact, the whole experience was so significant to me that I reserved them for only the most special occasions, and I'm pretty sure I never got as much use out of them as I should have. The impact their thoughtful gift had was broader than they may have ever thought and continues to produce fruit. To this day, one of the delights of my life is taking missionary kids, preacher boys, or young pastors to a good clothing store to get them clothes they might not normally be able to buy.

Another special memory happened much later, when Mimi and I were ten years into our ministry in northern Spain. One of the surprises God brought to us was an old Basque farmhouse we transformed into a Christian retreat center. Among the events we have hosted there are the intensive institutes, which now number 35. These full Saturday seminars began back in 1998 with a tiny group of believers in our little church building. Over the years, Dr. Garlock has taught three of these concentrated Bible courses, but a very special one occurred in June of 2002. It was the first to take place at the very rustic Aierdi farmhouse. Without inside plumbing, surrounded by old beams and rock walls, and obtaining power from a tiny generator, there could have been some reason for complaint. But nobody seemed in the least bit distracted by these minor matters, as Brother Frank walked us through the fascinating and stirring story of Ruth.

Mimi and I are very grateful for the friendship the Lord has given us with the Garlocks. They have enriched our lives and been an example to follow. It is our hope that by God's grace we will add to the story of grace that came to us when Dr. and Mrs. "G" walked into our lives.

— Andy and Mimi Bonikowsky

I would recommend that anyone reading this testimonial obtain both *The Aierdi Miracle* (published by CTS Publications) and *Just a Minute: Biblical Meditations in a Busy World* (published by Journey Forth, a division of Bob Jones University Press), two books written by Andy Bonikowsky. The first book tells how God works. The second book has a thorough organization of ideas that will strengthen your devotional life.

VIGNETTE 16

A LIFELONG RELATIONSHIP

ONE OF the blessings of just showing up as you follow the Lord's leading is the way he brings your life in contact with people who are experiencing sorrow. Sorrowing people sometimes just need someone to take an interest in them.

I am thinking of a story that I read many years ago about a little boy who lived with his mother across the street from an elderly couple. In the process of time, the elderly lady died and her husband was left alone. One day, the little boy's mother looked out the window and saw her little son sitting on the old man's lap on his front porch. When the boy came home later, his mother said: "What did you say to the old man?" The little boy replied, "I didn't say anything. I just helped him cry!"

That was what happened when Dr. Susan Kindall's mother passed away. Susan was only 17 years old. At that time, our two daughters, Shelly and Gina, were still rather young. Knowing how our girls would have felt if that had happened to their mother, Flora Jean and I cried right along with Susan. That was what began a lifelong relationship between Susan and us.

I really did not do very much for Susan. I believe it was the fact that I took an interest in this musically talented young girl that has encouraged her to develop her many outstanding talents. God has allowed Susan to use them to challenge, encourage, and be a blessing to many other Christian musicians, especially pianists.

Her students are successful international piano competition laureates, doctoral graduates of leading conservatories, performing/recording artists, and published composers. Many of her students have become teachers who chair university piano departments and direct ministries around the globe.

It has been a special joy for Flora Jean and me to watch Susan grow into the wonderful spiritual woman that she is today. We have followed her through high school, college, doctoral studies, and as Professor of Music and Piano Pedagogy at Bob Jones University. Many of her acquaintances have told us that she is the smartest person they have ever met, but her wisdom enables her to carry that intelligence with humility. In addition to this, God is also allowing us to meet many of the young musicians whom she is mentoring as they develop their talents under her skillful leadership. Susan testifies:

> My lifelong association with Dr. Frank Garlock began as a young girl in the 1970s, more than 40 years ago. I was privileged to grow up under his music ministry (with his wife, Flora Jean, as pianist) at Southside Baptist Church on Augusta Road in Greenville, South Carolina. Not until I traveled to hundreds of American churches as a pianist with Dr. Bob Jones III (president of Bob Jones University) did I realize how special our sacred music ministry at Southside really was.
>
> When I was a teenager, I assumed that, like the Garlocks, all church music directors wrote their own songs and weekly service music in the tradition of J. S. Bach, published their own hymnals and sacred music materials, and ministered to the community through weekly televised broadcasts. I also assumed that all church pianists virtually improvised

hymns at the highest concert level, wrote and published their own hymn improvisation instructional materials and arrangements, and released professional recordings. I thought that all church choirs were taught to read music and utilize proper classical vocal technique at rehearsals by the choir director and were recorded professionally as our Southside musicians were. The Garlocks continue to lead the way. Their *Majesty Hymns* and *Praises* books remain a constant in conservative, fundamental churches.

Dr. Garlock's artistic influence (as a composer, conductor, and performer fully dedicated to Christ) was a guiding light for me as a young 17-year-old musician who sang soprano solos, and then later composed, arranged, and performed sacred music. What makes Frank Garlock most singular among musicians is his personal walk with the Lord. The special blessing of God upon his life through music is like that of no other musician I know. It is a privilege to call him my friend. His godly mentoring influence continues to be a blessing in my life and the lives of my students and colleagues at BJU and abroad.

Faithful service to Christ is the heartbeat of this man's life. I have sought to emulate this in my own life. The titles of the Garlock's songs show this unhindered working of the Holy Spirit in his heart—*I Want to Be Faithful, My Life Is Thine, Keep Walking With the Lord, He Cares For You, To Love Is To Give, There Is a Way, He's So Great, The God of All Comfort, I Belong to Jesus, Do Right, I Am Trusting Thee Lord Jesus, Give Me This Mountain, Jesus Is Lord, Confession, He Walks Beside Me*, and many others.

His consistent testimony continues to be an influence beyond measure, not only in my life, but also in the lives of my students and colleagues throughout the world. Dr. Garlock inspires others to give their all for Jesus Christ by openly living this truth. Since his unstinting support during my early days of doctoral work at The University of Oklahoma even until now, as I serve the Lord as the founder and director of the Majesty Music Academy, Frank Garlock remains a dynamic encourager.

Throughout my life Dr. Garlock has been both my musical father and my second spiritual father, especially now in the stead of my own biological dad who went to heaven on Thanksgiving Day 2014. As Dr. Garlock often reminds me, "the natural response of a joyful Christian heart in fellowship with the Lord is to sing." Praising God through sunshine and rain, his life and music exemplify God's grace, strength, joy and bring hope for tomorrow.

—*Dr. Susan Kindall*

VIGNETTE 17

A LONG BUS RIDE

D R. DAVID Ledgerwood is the Chair of the Music Department of Maranatha Baptist University in Watertown, Wisconsin. The Chamber Singers that he conducts is an outstanding group that demonstrates the things that he is teaching them in his academic music courses. This allows him to watch God work in the lives of his students.

I call this vignette "A Long Bus Ride" since it illustrates so effectively the kind of thing a young person who wants to serve the Lord will probably have to do. A person who wants to serve the Lord must be willing to be in training for the long haul. When David mentions his long bus ride, he at the time was ministering at a small church and Christian school in Clymer, Pennsylvania. He and his family were living in a small trailer behind the church and sacrificing to serve the Lord.

David's willingness to cash in an insurance policy and make the long trip to Pensacola Christian College demonstrates the character trait that is now making him so effective in training others. He sacrificed to come to the Pensacola summer master's program after the Lord opened the door for me to administer it. This summer program allowed me to help those who were either teaching in a Christian school or serving in a local church and wanted to obtain a Master's Degree in Sacred Music at the same time.

While David was attending the Master's program at PCC, he wrote a beautiful accompaniment to one of our songs that is still one of our favorites: "All I Have Belongs to Jesus." This song was originally written for our daughter Gina's wedding in 1985, and Flora Jean and I have sung it many times as a duet at other weddings. Its original title was "All We Have Belongs to Jesus" [see figure 2]. I even recorded this song on my solo album after I orchestrated the wonderful accompaniment that David wrote. Here is how God has led this man:

I enlisted in an Air Force field band in 1973 after three semesters as a piano major in college. My duties included playing piano for the jazz trio, stage band, and Dixieland band, keyboard for the rock band, and percussion for the concert and marching bands. My spiritual background was religious, but I did not have a personal relationship with Christ.

The man I was to replace in the service (Mike), was a Christian who was dedicated after getting his life right with the Lord. Mike felt that some of the music he was asked to perform was not in harmony with his Christian walk, and so he was glad to pass it off to me. Mike talked to me constantly about his faith: and as I viewed Mike's transparent walk with the Lord, I began to see myself as a sinner.

One night on a trip to a different part of the state, I came under conviction and Mike pointed me to Christ. I received the Lord, kneeling down beside my bed. Mike then introduced me to a Serviceman's Center near our base where weekly Bible studies were held. It was during one of those Bible studies, in 1974, that I heard tapes of Frank Garlock speaking about music. It was refreshing to hear someone with music credentials speak about music and the Christian life. As a young Christian, that was the combination to which I aspired.

After leaving the service, completing my undergraduate music degree, and accepting a position in a Christian school, I heard of a Master's Program directed by Dr. Garlock. I had always wanted to study with him, and so this seemed to be the perfect chance.

I cashed in a life insurance policy and rode 27 long hours on a bus to begin the three-week course. It turned out to be a wonderful time of challenge and fellowship. Dr. Garlock's courses in Choral Arranging, Conducting, and the History of Sacred Music were especially memorable. His teaching was inspiring, and I desperately wanted to improve. I considered my presence in the program a sacred trust from the Lord and thus gave my studies full attention.

With very little background in non-liturgical church music, much was new to me. As I listened to Mrs. Garlock play her arrangements and improvise, I wondered where in the world she "got those sounds." As I took lessons from her, she challenged me to not be careless with my hymn-playing, but to play with heartfelt expression, striving to focus on the meaning of the text.

Many years later I am now in a leadership position. I am the teacher for classes in Choral Arranging and Hymnology. I regularly conduct a choral group. I teach improvisation, and I am a church pianist and organist. I work with new students each year, challenging each one to consider a

Christian perspective on artistic expression and help them understand that a biblical foundation is non-optional, regardless of talent. These were all things I first learned from the Garlocks.

Thank you, Dr. and Mrs. Garlock, for your investment in me. My desire is that it will continually bear fruit to God's glory.

—Dr. David Ledgerwood

VIGNETTE 18

THE GREAT CONDUCTOR

I HAVE always admired and respected John Vaughn, even before he became Dr. Vaughn. When he first came to Greenville, he joined Southside Baptist Church, and attended the Sunday school class I taught there. For 30 years, he was the pastor of a struggling group of believers that is now the eminent fundamental Faith Baptist Church in Taylors, South Carolina. Also, I knew him as the man who faced a family tragedy that would have disheartened and destroyed most men. He trusted God, rose above the difficulty, and used the tragedy to build not only a great church to the glory of God, but to establish a ministry for others who face what may seem like insurmountable difficulties.

I asked my friend in the ministry to outline the path that the Lord has brought him through. I wanted to let the readers of this book see how God has given him the grace and the strength to face his trials and still, to this day, be the victorious Christian that I know him to be. It is still amazing to me that two days before the fire in the Vaughn's home which changed his family for years to come, Ron Hamilton lost his eye to cancer. Both events have given these men ministries that they never could have imagined because of their response to what happened in their lives and their complete trust in God in spite of the circumstances.

I am trusting the Lord will use the following testimony to help many others follow Dr. Vaughn's example and watch God fulfill His will for them just as He did for this man of God. I would also suggest that anyone reading this testimony should obtain the book *More Precious than Gold: The Fiery Trial of a Family's Faith,* by John and Brenda Vaughn, published originally by Fleming H. Revell Company and now available from the John C. Vaughn Evangelistic Association, Inc. at www.johncvaughn.com.

In late August 1975 my wife and I arrived in Greenville to finish college. We had met in 1966 as students at Cumberland College in Williamsburg, Kentucky, where we both had enrolled on music scholarships to study Music Education. After our first year of study we were engaged, and we planned to be married after graduation. But in early 1968, the Tet Offensive in Vietnam changed not only the course of that war but of the next seven years of our lives. When I joined the Air Force that year, our music education was set aside. During my second tour of duty in Southeast Asia, I came to Christ through the faithful witness of two soul winners. When I returned home, we were led to a church pastored by a graduate of Bob Jones University, Pastor Tom Harper. Although I was a new Christian, I knew I was called to preach. Following our new pastor's advice, we set off for BJU. He had also told us, "Don't visit every church in town; just join Southside." So we did, with our third child on the way.

On our first Sunday there, we could see the piano from our seats and stared in amazement as Mrs. Garlock literally played, it seemed, the entire piano. When Dr. Frank Garlock got up to teach our first Couples Serving Christ (CSC) Sunday school class, I realized why God had sent us to Southside. The pastor was wise and kind and often preached very long sermons. Over the ensuing years, those who listened to me preach for an hour or more had no idea how inspired I had been at Southside!

Although I would not recommend it to others, immediately after graduation I accepted the pastorate of a small group meeting held in a little metal building in a textile mill village on the west side of Greenville. Pastor Handford had given me the same advice I would have given a novice in such an impossible situation, "It could be an opportunity to gain some experience, but you realize you won't be able to make it a long term ministry." We had only been at Southside for two years. Thus, in the fall of 1977, I became a pastor. However, by God's grace, our little group became a real church which prospered and grew. Now after thirty years of pastoring this local church, advanced degrees completed through the patience of those dear people, and eight years as an evangelist, I am still a member there. In fact, today the Garlocks are also members of this same church, and together we sit under the skillful biblical teaching of our pastor, Dr. John Monroe. I am the Pastor Emeritus now, and Dr. Garlock is active in many areas of the ministry including still playing his trombone in the church orchestra. Dr. Tim Fisher, the long-time Minister of Music is holding the standard high as Dr. Garlock did when I sat under his ministry at Southside years ago. I have often talked with them about the fact that Faith is today what Southside was forty years ago. And if that is so, it is because we simply set the course we learned there and stayed that course.

Perhaps the reader will ask, "Indeed, what were you thinking? How could anyone have learned to teach and preach the Bible with just two years of Bible college and so little time even to have attended a good church?" No doubt it had more to do with enthusiasm than education and more to do with military discipline than true discipleship, but there was far more life-changing truth coming into our lives in those two short years of initial preparation than would ever have been possible were it not for Frank Garlock. Dr. Tom Harper has always been a Bible teacher, and he knew what I needed and would receive at Southside. Similarly, although Dr. Garlock is known around the world for his incredible impact through music, he too is primarily a Bible teacher. He not only teaches music on a biblical foundation, he teaches far more than music by teaching the Bible. As the great apostle said in 1 Peter 4:11, "If any man speak, let him speak as the oracles of God; if any man minister, let him do it as of the ability which God **giveth**: that God in all things may be glorified through Jesus Christ, to whom be praise and dominion for ever and ever. Amen."

The word "giveth" is key. It is the word from which we derive "chorus," and it speaks of the choral director who supplies all that the chorus requires to correctly sing their individual parts. I can think of no better verse to summarize the ministry of Dr. Frank Garlock.

Perhaps the reader should know that at Southside we were unable to be in the choir or participate in special music. We were in school full-time; I was working full-time; we had two young children and a baby on the way. What we learned was learned in Sunday school and as we participated in congregational singing—which was always a short seminar on singing. Through his teaching we came to see our very lives as the song we sing to the glory of God. We were not just learning more about Christian music; we were learning more about Christ.

When we were at Southside in the mid-seventies, the Southside Baptist Church Choir was probably the best church choir in existence, certainly within the circles in which we moved. Our background in music (studying its theory, history, and performance) brought us to Dr. Garlock's weekly lessons with hearts and minds ready to respond to his clear, convicting, practical, funny, warm instruction that made each lesson worth more than we could ever have imagined. It is not an exaggeration to say that every thought he presented was an "Ah-ha!" moment for us. We came with a seemingly unlimited number of questions and soon realized that the Bible is a book of un-limited answers. Thus, we were quickly grounded in the critically important truth that the best way to become a grounded, discerning Christian is to be exposed to regular teaching and application of the Bible. I determined in the CSC class that if God would, in fact, allow me to become a pastor that the two essentials of my ministry would be sound Bible teaching with clear application and excellent music that was fit for its true audience: the Lord Himself.

Specifically, one of the most valuable lessons I learned in those days is that each one of us has a "life message" which is our God-given testimony—our song—that we share with others through our words and our example. That teaching has prepared so many for a Christ-honoring response to God-ordained circumstances we would never choose apart from Him. Recently, Dr. Garlock gave me a recording of his lesson in the CSC class given on May 21, 1978. I had been the pastor of Faith Baptist for just seven months. He opened the class that day as always by sharing prayer requests. The first request was for my family. He spoke of the life-changing fire in our home just the night before that would begin a long struggle for survival for my wife and our little daughter, Becky. They continued to pray for us for years. In fact, they prayed for Brenda until the Lord took her home on September 2, 2013, from complications related to the fire so long ago. The Garlocks continue to pray for Becky and me today. The second request was for Ron Hamilton, the Garlocks' son-in-law, who on that Thursday, two days before our fire, had lost his eye in surgery due to cancer.

Like these two examples, the many connections between truth and trials are, in a sense, God's applications of His great sermon, the Bible. It is certainly no coincidence that God gives us His Word to prepare us for trials, to sustain us in trials, and to deepen our life message through those trials. Just a month before the fire, my Sunday evening sermon was "The Crucible of Christian Suffering," taken from the two verses that follow the one quoted above: "Beloved, think it not strange concerning the fiery trial which is to try you, as though some strange thing happened unto you: But rejoice, inasmuch as ye are partakers of Christ's sufferings; that, when His glory shall be revealed, ye may be glad also with exceeding joy." 1 Peter 4:12-13.

That summer, on a return trip from visiting my wife in the hospital in Charleston, I stopped by Southside to give an update on her and our daughter who was in a hospital in Cincinnati, Ohio. I was humbled and blessed that day to hear a recording of Ron singing during the previous Sunday morning service. Of course, it was his signature song, "Rejoice in the Lord," sung there for the first time in public. As I listened to his rich, resonant voice, it was as though he was ministering to me personally; "God never moves without purpose or plan, when trying His servant and molding a man." The chosen verse of my senior class at BJU had been Job 23:10, "But He knoweth the way that I take: when He hath tried me, I shall come forth as gold." Years later, Brenda and I wrote a book titled *More Precious than Gold*, telling the story of the fire and the ministry of special education we founded, Hidden Treasure Christian School. Our title was taken from 1 Peter 1:7, "That the trial of your faith, being much more precious than of gold that perisheth, though it be tried with fire, might be found unto praise and honour and glory at the appearing of Jesus Christ."

With permission, we reprinted the words and music to Ron's song in the back of that book, along with a picture of Becky at age ten sitting with Ron, who was dressed as "Patch the Pirate." Through radio, television, books, recordings, the internet, and unnumbered Christians serving in sermon and song, these intertwined testimonies have reached untold millions around the world. Whenever we were asked to sign a Bible or a book, Brenda always wrote the reference "Job 23:10," and I wrote "1 Peter 4:12-13."

Behind the stories of this unique ministry of music that has, so far, reached two generations of children and adults and this unique ministry of special education that has reached students that no other school could help, is the unseen hand of Frank Garlock—his life, his lessons, his love urging us on. As we know from both the Bible and experience, the greatness of the chorus and orchestra is the greatness of the conductor. One Christmas season, Dr. Tim Fisher and his wife Debbie took us to a live performance in Atlanta where from our front row center seats we were enthralled by the masterful artistry of the great conductor Robert Shaw. We listened and watched as he evoked the sound from the musicians with the skillful movements of his hands. I share that to say that we have studied and seen excellence. It is evident to me that Dr. Garlock is also a great conductor. It is a fact that his life and ministry exude excellence. But more importantly, through his instruction and example over four decades, we have been learning more and more to follow, not him, but the Great Conductor of All of Life, adding our voices—our song—to the great symphony of praise offered by all who truly know and love Him.

—Dr. John C. Vaughn

VIGNETTE 19

CREATING A PERFECT TAPESTRY

I AM always amazed when I think of the people who have crossed my path who have accomplished so much for the Lord in their relative fields, particularly in the area of music. Joan Jacobson Pinkston is one of those people.

Joan has published numerous sacred choral pieces, primarily with SoundForth and Beckenhorst Press. In 2002, Joan's 816-page hymnbook, *Hymns of Grace and Glory*, was published and features more than seventy of her own hymn tunes. During her 40 years as a professional musician, she has published over 400 pieces of music, given over a hundred workshops on composing and arranging, and performed numerous sacred concerts. She has also written five film scores.

Mrs. Pinkston has taught music theory, hymn improvisation, orchestration, and choral composition at Bob Jones University for more than 48 years. Many of her former students are currently involved in writing, publishing, and performing sacred music.

When this composer was my student in Sophomore Music Theory, I recognized at that time that she had a special gift because of the quality of work she did for her class assignments. I knew she would someday produce outstanding original compositions and sacred music arrangements. As I quoted Dr. Gustafson in the preface of this book, teaching Joan Pinkston was "one of those wonderful, unplanned moments . . . that glowed like a candle in the dark" for me.

Here is Joan's portrayal of our relationship which she has woven into a "perfect tapestry" that shows how God can use anyone who will show up and be faithful in the place He has led them:

The older one gets, it becomes more and more marvelous to see how the hand of God has arranged life's journey. The people that are placed with us along our pilgrim pathway are exactly those that are needed to shape us into the servants that the Lord desires us to be for His own glory. It is like our lives are woven together to create a perfect tapestry, each thread necessary to completing the whole.

As I look back, I see that before college the Lord was giving me tools to equip me for what was in store for His calling for me. These tools were mainly an excellent background in piano and cello playing, a good start in music theory training, a wide exposure to classical music, and parents who, though untrained in music themselves, were sacrificially willing to help and encourage me in all of the former pursuits.

When I got to college, the Lord gradually and lovingly changed my aspirations to become involved in music theory and composition. It was Dr. Frank Garlock who inspired me and encouraged me in this transition. He became my true mentor; and his help, encouragement, and friendship has only grown over these fifty years. His teaching, enthusiasm, and godly spirit have always been an immense influence and challenge to me. In a technical sense, he not only gave me a firm grounding harmonically and analytically, but he also taught me that every musical line—every vocal part, every instrumental part—must be carefully crafted for melodic excellence and integrity. This has been the most important aspect of my writing and teaching.

As our life's tapestry unfolds, a most remarkable design may be perceived. It is remarkable to see how God has used my ministry to be a constant extension of Dr. Garlock's ministry. I will only cite a couple examples. Dr. Garlock taught me, but then I taught all of his children and several of his grandchildren. Juan Marcos Martinez [Vignette 22] is one of the many students that Dr. Garlock has aided in order to make college a reality. Juan Marcos worked diligently as an undergraduate student and became a composition major in graduate school. I was privileged to teach Juan Marcos for five years in college, and now he is teaching music theory and composition in his hometown in Mexico. All of my students are Dr. Garlock's "grand-students," and there are many hundreds of them. His own efforts have taken him to teach many students across the globe; my students are adding to that number by ministering in the Philippines, Russia, Germany, Singapore, Australia, Mexico and other places. Around twenty-five former students have become published composers. Another twenty-five are teaching music theory in America or abroad.

It is amazing to see how the Lord can multiply the gifts and labors of one dedicated servant. The ministry of Dr. Garlock has been very far reaching, and the half of it is not even known. Thank you, Dr. Garlock, for enabling me and so many others to serve Christ to the best of our abilities.

May God be glorified as we use His good gifts to exalt His holy name.

Your ever-grateful student and friend,

—*Joan J. Pinkston*

I want to include here my analysis of a short example of Joan's work to try to explain why I believe in Joan's extraordinary abilities. In 1978, Joan set to music some profound thoughts about how to worship God in song. These thoughts are encapsulated in a poem called "My Song" by Dr. Bob Jones Jr., president of BJU at that time. The resulting hymn is only 16 measures long and it is what C. H. Spurgeon would have called a quintessential "Jewel of Praise."

I realize that some of my readers will not understand the technical musical analysis, but I believe that trained musicians will, so I am addressing this particularly to them. I am adding a picture of the hymn to this book, with the measures numbered, so that each person can see what I am writing about [see figure 3]. By the way, I should say here that Joan's husband Bill says that Joan writes the music and then I analyze what she wrote. (That is my job as a music theorist.) Please notice, even if you do not understand all the technical jargon, how masterfully Joan paints and colors the beautiful words that Dr. Jones wrote.

I would also like to suggest that you play this hymn on your piano (even if you are like me and not a good pianist); or better yet, get a group of any size together and sing this hymn in four parts to get the full impact of the message, beauty and masterful word painting by Joan Jacobson Pinkston.

A Simple Analysis of Masterful Word Painting

I. The use of the C Major chord.

    A. The first five counts are built on this chord.

        1. Measure 1 is all in C with non-harmonics to emphasize "Thou" and especially "joy."

        2. The bass is a C pedal point for that measure.

        3. It begins in open structure (more than an octave between the melody and the tenor) to have a written-into-the-music crescendo into measure 2.

    B. Measure 2 begins with a C chord in closed structure.

        1. Everything thus far is leading up to that chord.

        2. It accentuates (turns the light on) the word "Joy."

    C. Measure 3 leads into the C chord in first inversion on count 3 to highlight the first syllable of the word "angel."

    D. Measure 6 leads up to the C chord with a 7-6 suspension to highlight the first syllable of the word "silent," with added perfect stress that uses the melodic leap of a fifth down on that word.

    E. Measure 13 uses the C chord in first inversion to accent the first syllable of the word "sinner."

    F. Measure 14 is *a most dramatic use* of the C chord in root position with a minor 7th to emphasize "saved" that is the *key word* of the song. (Anyone familiar with Handel's *Messiah*, or with Haydn's *Creation* will recognize the use of this device to indicate the climactic close of one of the work's extended choruses. Mrs. Pinkston judiciously did this on measure 14 of this short work.)

    G. Measure 15 uses the C chord in 2nd inversion to highlight "cause."

II. The use of the E major sound for color.

    A. Measure 5 begins on E major to open the beginning of the second line.

1. To begin a phrase on this chord is startling.
2. This could be a III$^{\#5}$ chord in C Major, or it could be considered a temporary modulation into A minor. Either way, it paints "stammering" perfectly, and the addition of the 4-3 suspension on the A minor chord followed by the embellished 7th in measure 6 completes the thought in coloring the word "stammering."

B. Measure 7 uses the same chord in first inversion on the word "owe," to tie the entire phrase together.

C. The use of the E Major sound with an added 7th in first inversion on the word "while" in measure 11 as the phrase is building is ideally placed.

D. Transforming the sound to an E minor chord to begin the last line skillfully sets up the C Major chord with a minor 7th in the next measure for the word "saved."

III. The use of the 7th chords (Mm7, m7, hd7, dim7 & MmM9)

Mm7— Major/minor 7th (Major triad, minor 7th)
m7— minor triad, minor 7th
hd7— half-diminished 7th (diminished triad, minor 7th)
dim7— diminished triad and diminished 7th
MmM9— Major triad, minor 7th, Major 9th

A. Measure 1 contains the word "Whom," which is lightly emphasized by the use of a hd7 chord over the C pedal. (The hd7 could be two lower neighbors and one upper neighbor.)

B. Measure 3 uses the m7 chord in first inversion to lightly emphasize the word "Whom" again.

C. Measure 4 uses the MmM9 chord (II^9#4 or secondary dominant) with double accented passing tones on the next count to beautifully color "adore."

D. Measure 6 uses the hd7 to prepare the mind for the word "silent."

E. Measure 7 begins with a m7 chord that prepares the way for the "open" m7 in first inversion to emphasize "<u>so</u> much more" in measure 8.

F. Measure 9 begins the next phrase with a Mm7 in 2nd inversion to start another written-in-the-music crescendo that is genius. The whole line is built around the verb "swell" in measure 10. Also, this whole phrase is full of 7th chords that lead up to the MmM9 that comes in measure 12 to reach a pinnacle on the word "<u>prais</u>es." The entire phrase culminates on a Mm7 with a 4-3 suspension to relax the tension of the crescendo.

G. The last phrase that begins on an E minor chord in first inversion (a III chord) makes generous use of 7th chords. The second count of measure 13 is a Mm7 in 3rd inversion that becomes a hd7 in 2nd inversion on the last half of count two on "a" to lead into "sinner" and a Mm7 in 2nd inversion on count 4 that leads into the dramatic Mm7 on the tonic in measure 14 to emphatically highlight the word "saved," a Mm7 chord in first inversion in measure 14 to point up the first syllable of the word "<u>par</u>doned, the dim7 in measure 15 to accent the word "more," and the final Mm7 with a 4-3 suspension in the final measure to point out that the angels (the word "they") will have to listen to the saints sing of redemption because they are not redeemed beings.

Much more could be said about this jewel of soul-stirring poetry written by Dr. Bob Jones Jr. that was set to music by one of the great composers of sacred music today. You can probably tell that I am still exercising my gift of teaching in this vignette. However, I want to close this analysis by commenting that I believe very few people can really appreciate this sixteen-measure masterpiece of poetry and music. I am glad that Majesty Music has included this hymn in all three hymnals that we have published, including *Himnos Majestuosos,* our Spanish hymnal. Not recognizing its worth, other hymnals did not include the hymn. It is unfortunate that a musically trained committee of editors would inadvertently overlook this stellar jewel of Christian hymnody. I hope that this vignette will help readers of this book to recognize its biblical, poetic, and musical value and incorporate it into their congregational singing.

Before we leave a discussion of this hymn, I want to relate an opportunity the Lord gave me to show up in an unusual way. Dr. Susan Kindall invited an internationally known pianist and musicologist to give a lecture at BJU on September 21, 2013.

After the lecture, Dr. Kindall invited me to meet with the two of them and a few BJU piano students for lunch at a local restaurant. Knowing that the visiting guest was not saved, and probably did not know the quality of the faculty at the university, I decided to take several copies of Joan's hymn to the lunch and use it to share her outstanding composition skills with the visitor.

After I showed the visiting guest how skillfully Mrs. Pinkston musically painted the words of this hymn, Dr. Kindall pulled me aside as we left the restaurant and said: "You just gave her the gospel!" Because this artist and music scholar could relate to the technical expertise of the music, she received a clear explanation of what it means to become a Christian. Only eternity will reveal whether the truth planted in this woman's heart will bear fruit, but God allowed me to use this unusual opportunity to plant some spiritual seed for His glory.

I would like to close this vignette with part of a letter I wrote to Joan after Flora Jean and I heard her play some of her hymn arrangements at The Logos Theatre in Taylors, South Carolina on March 8, 2009.

Dear Joan:

I had to write and tell you how much Flora Jean and I enjoyed the program of hymns this afternoon. Your arrangements and your piano playing were both fantastic and the whole program was a tremendous blessing. We both cried at the beauty of the music that was written and performed to bring glory to our wonderful Savior who deserves only the best we can give Him. May the Lord continue to bless you, give you strength, and allow you to use the wonderful talent He has given you for many years to come.

VIGNETTE 20

JEWELS OF PRAISE

I AM calling this next vignette "Jewels of Praise" after something that C. H. Spurgeon wrote years ago: "Let us weave His mercies into a song. Let us take the pure gold of thankfulness, and the *jewels of praise* and make them into another crown for the head of Jesus." What Dr. Dana Everson says in this next essay is another "Jewel of Praise" that I want to include in this book. God brought Dana across my path thirty-one years ago as I literally just showed up to encourage him to become the musician and the man that God intended for him to be.

How I Started Out in Music

At age 13, I played in a bar for the first time. Don't ask me how I got to work there in the first place . . . possibly because I knew all the old tunes from the big band era and I always looked older than my years. Perhaps the dark, smoke-filled room hid me well as I sat quite unobtrusively behind the old upright grand piano. My ear and improvisational skills were more than enough to allow me to play in the clubs and bars for the next 10 years or so. I paid most of my way through college by playing for parties and proms, with older musicians as well as performers of my own age. I had memorized hundreds of popular, rock, swing, and jazz songs. I played saxophone, clarinet, trumpet, and keyboard instruments in several bands. I arranged for pop, jazz, marching bands, and swing bands all before I was a senior in college. I never cared for the liquor but became addicted to the commercial performance atmo-sphere, the applause, the easy money, and especially to the music itself.

I was searching, however, for a higher purpose in life than living for Saturday night parties (with Sunday morning headaches). I had always believed there was a personal God, but I felt far away from Him as the mysterious ritu-als of my church seemed to add layers of formalities and ceremonies that did more to separate my relationship with the Lord than draw me to know Him personally. But because I had a sincere desire to know God, He began to send people into my life to confront me with the simple Gospel of salvation. The most important influence was the life and testimony of the girl I later married, Gloria Ortega, who was a music student at Michigan State University. After much restlessness and inward struggle, I told the Lord I had made a mess of my life and asked Him to save me. That day, He began a long journey with me in which He started to transform every part of my life, including that which I had loved most, music.

I was mentored by some fine musical performers, com-posers, and music teachers through my teens and early twenties. I had also been mentored by some godly spiri-tual leaders after my conversion in 1973. But it wasn't until nearly ten years after my salvation decision that I met an extraordinary, godly person who was also an extraordinarily skilled musician.

How I Was Convinced That I Met a New Hero

When my wife and I went to enroll our oldest son in our Christian school, the principal informed everyone that listening to rock music was not allowed. (At the time, I was writing for and directing a college stage band. I no longer played in nightclubs and bar rooms because I realized the atmosphere was contrary to Christian growth. However, I continued to play most of the same music, not considering the possible ramifications of the musical styles.) I asked the principal, "how would you define 'rock music'?" He said, "I'm not sure, but here is a resource which explains a lot about Bible principles of music." He loaned me THE SYMPHONY OF LIFE audio tapes . . . and I was floored. I had never before thought of music as moral or immoral. I knew music had emotional influence and could produce an atmosphere, but I was dumbfounded at the realization that it could influence a person's thinking and spiritual life!

Outside of my family, I have a few "heroes"—people who stand with integrity for what God has called them to do. The Garlocks have become such heroes to me since I met them in 1984.

Dr. Garlock did not dodge my questions. He patiently answered every question I had with reasoned and practical responses. Now here was someone that could give biblical reasons not only for his philosophy of sacred music, but for music in general. By his teaching, writing, and personal encouragement, I saw so much to imitate and pass on to my students.

He pointed to Scripture first, then to music theory, music history, and performance practices. He could perform, conduct, teach, compose, and preach. He had boundless energy and a passion for his calling. He was obviously a man of purpose and drive. That alone would be inspiring to anyone who is willing to discipline himself to learn from him. These were exactly the skills and character traits I admired and had sensed that God wanted to develop in my life. So, I found a new hero.

He was totally honest. He believed what he said he believed. Integrity is a quality that is absolutely essential in any ministry situation. He didn't ask his students to do what he was unwilling to do or had not already done. He was inspiring. Teaching is more than conveying facts. It involves passing on attitudes, motivating students, and demonstrating a passion for excellence. I found these qualities at the feet of both Frank and Flora Jean Garlock.

He mentored me in ways he will probably never realize. For example, there was a certain humility that I saw, despite his extensive musical training at the revered Eastman School of Music under some of the finest teachers in America. There was no pretense. Demand for diligence? Yes! Strong challenges to keep improving? Certainly! Courage to stand for what he believed in? Absolutely! But no arrogance. Anyone who seriously studies the man will find that he "bragged on God's grace," if you please.

After digesting the materials Dr. Garlock presented in his lectures and books and after meeting him and watching his testimony, I began to incorporate many of the principles he had sifted from the Scriptures. I blended these principles into the materials I taught in music theory, music history, private lessons, and music philosophy courses. I have strived to urge my students to do more than merely entertain and to use their music abilities primarily to minister and edify others in their local churches, families, and communities. Music is a form of worship—expressing attitude, atmosphere, and beliefs.

To be a musician at any level requires diligence, skill, and purpose as presented in the Scriptures. I now have published about 500 sacred instrumental arrangements intended for use in churches and schools. I dedicated my book *Sound Roots* to Dr. Garlock because of the lasting impact and encouragement he has produced in my life and work. Truly, here is a man who continues to influence my thinking, my teaching, and my love for mentoring others to develop their musical skills to further the ministry of the gospel. Much of whatever I have accomplished in writing, performing, and teaching sacred music in the past 30+ years has been stimulated by his consistent ministry.

—*Dr. Dana F. Everson*

Dr. Everson could have been a respected musician and entertainer in any field he had chosen. He is also an outstanding composer and arranger. (When he attended a master's class on arranging that I was teaching on the topic of arranging, I asked the class to write a simple melody and counterpoint just to see what they knew. Dana turned in a whole new choir arrangement on his original melody the next day.) He is a quintessential saxophonist; he can lie on his back on a piano bench and play the piano upside-down; he has been an excellent teacher of college students majoring in music for 33 years; and he is willing to do whatever God calls him to do. I believe his life and ministry is definitely *another jewel for the crown for the head of Jesus.*

I would also like to suggest that anyone reading this should obtain a copy of Dr. Everson's book, *Sound Roots, Steps to Building a Biblical Philosophy of Music.* This book was his doctoral dissertation and is published by Bible Revival Ministries, 114 Briarview Circle, Greenville, SC, 29615. It is a well-thought-out and documented treatise that pastors, and especially music ministers, should read and have in their libraries.

VIGNETTE 21

MY LIFE IS THINE

D R. MIKE Zachary is exceptional in several fields including music. He has many abilities. He is an excellent pianist,
music arranger, composer, organizer, educator, administrator, author, and editor. As you can see from the letter below to me, he is a
godly encourager. In addition to all his other degrees, Mike holds a
Doctor of Musical Arts in Piano from the American Conservatory
of Music in Chicago.

He is another person, like several others in this book, whom I esteem
as being "one of the smartest people I have ever met, but whose wisdom enables him to carry that intelligence with humility." In fact,
as I was teaching Music Theory in the master's degree program in
Pensacola Christian College, many of the students had difficulty in
that area because they were not trained properly in the school where
they received their bachelor's degree. I suggested to many students that
they take Music Theory by correspondence from Mike. I then said:
"If he passes you, so do I!" That is how much confidence I have in Dr.
Zachary's ability to teach what is needed, even by correspondence,
which is unbelievably difficult.

Let me tell you why I call this vignette "My Life Is Thine." The occa-
sion was a time when, before I was to speak, I was told that at least
half of the people there did not want to hear my message. The words
of this song came directly from my heart as I knelt before God by
the bed in my motel room and pleaded with the Lord to help me

[see figure 4]. Here is what Mike wrote to me thirteen years after I wrote this song:

> *I was just playing "My Life Is Thine," and I began to wonder about the characteristics of a man who would pen such a set of words. I certainly couldn't write a psychological essay about the author; but my meditation did reveal to me that the kind of man who would write such a set of words is one who merits my deepest admiration and respect.*

Next is Dr. Mike Zachary's testimony about hearing one of my messages in 1984:

> In the little town of Hazen, North Dakota where life went by with predictable monotony, it was news when a new pastor came to our church. I was happy because he had a son about my age, and we soon became friends. One day, he brought an album to my house so we could listen to it, just to have something to do. It was *The Big Beat* by Dr. Frank Garlock.
>
> At that time in my life, I was receiving some attention for my academics, yet so many of the churches I had known were churches where academics and education were not overly important. Satan tempted me to believe that I needed to choose between my faith and academic excellence.
>
> Though *The Big Beat* presented Dr. Garlock's teaching on musical philosophy, my primary thought was, "I can't believe this. Here is a highly educated Christian. I didn't know you could be educated to this level and still serve in Christian ministry." The Lord began to show me that

a choice for Christianity was not destined to be a choice for ignorance.

I later learned that there had been a technical issue with the production company, and a high percentage of those albums had been damaged. Years later, the Garlocks told me, "If you listened to that album, we heard it first. We opened every single one of those to make sure they were right." To me, that was an important testimony about the importance of thoroughness. If my North Dakota buddy had brought a defective album to my house, we wouldn't have listened to it; and I might never have met the Garlocks.

When I learned that Dr. Garlock was leading a master's program at Pensacola Christian College, I remembered the album; and I jumped at the opportunity to attend. It was there at PCC that I met the Garlocks in person for the first time, and I took it all in like a sponge.

I still remember the times when Dr. Garlock spent time with me one-on-one. In working with me on one of my composition assignments, he penciled in a few changes, quietly demonstrating some important relationships that I had overlooked. Here was a man who had taken every single music theory course that Eastman School of Music offered, and he seemed to enjoy sharing his immense knowledge with me in a way I could understand.

Dr. Garlock is a man of enthusiasm, a skilled musician, a passionate preacher, and a man who invests in people. To my amazement, he also became one of my friends. Through the years, we talked about everything from the use of augmented sixth chords to how we can trust in the faithfulness of God, even when the situations of our lives seem hopeless.

Some years ago, I was at a restaurant with the Garlocks, and he began to share with me some of the personal struggles his family had endured. When he first began to answer my inquiry about how things were going, Mrs. Garlock said, "Oh, Frank, don't!"

But Dr. Garlock said, "No. Mike has asked me, and I'm going to tell him." As he began to explain some of the difficulties they had experienced, I fully grasped the idea that he is not a positive, energetic man because his life is utopian. He is a positive, energetic man because, when life was difficult, he leaned all the more on the Lord; and his passion for music and for preaching is a reflection of God's grace in his life.

His testimony caused me to reflect deeply on what it means to have a relationship with the Lord; and as my wife and I have navigated through some very deep waters, I have been inspired by the memory of his words, "Mike, through it all, God has been faithful."

Dr. Garlock has been a faithful steward of the multifold talents and abilities that God has given him. Whether he was quietly and carefully grading music theory papers, teaching a private trombone lesson, or speaking about the philosophy of music on a national platform, he has been diligent, faithful, and honest. Because of that, God was pleased to give him global influence. It is actually quite difficult to imagine the reach of this one man's life. Dr. Garlock's impact is a vivid reminder of the good that can be accomplished when God blesses our efforts.

For more than thirty years, I worked in Bible colleges as a music instructor. Now, I am serving in the music ministry of an outstanding church in Southern California. Though many years have passed, I still retain my teenage awe of this man, a man who is all man, a music man, and a man of God. Because Dr. Garlock is a spirit-filled man, his impact on my life always brought me closer to Christ. For this, and for his many other outstanding qualities, I will be eternally grateful.

—Dr. Mike Zachary

I would also like to quote something that Mike wrote as he was ready to receive his doctor's degree. This shows the sterling character of the man! It is titled: "Who Earned The Degree?"

My lovely wife has been rather eager to share the good news that her husband of ten years is finally out of school! I feel duty bound to set the record straight. While I was doing my little assignments in the classroom, my dear wife was making the greatest sacrifice. I guess no one can understand Angie's sacrifice unless they have experienced a similar situation. Angela was my Rock of Gibraltar, a constant tower of strength. She has merited my undying gratitude. Now that I have finished school, some may congratulate me. It would be better, though, to shower praise and honor on my wife. Though the Conservatory will confer a degree on me, it belongs to Angie.

I can relate with Mike's statement because of all the times that Flora Jean sacrificed for me to get my education, especially at the Eastman School of Music.

I could list some of the awards that Mike has received—including the fact that his grade average was 4.0 as he worked on his doctorate. I believe Mike Zachary's overriding character traits are his love for the Lord, his love for his wife, coupled with his desire to serve others and to be generous to the Nth degree. When he came to Pensacola to work on another master's degree, he brought flowers and candy for Flora Jean and an expensive tie for me. He then he invited us to go out for dinner with him on the first day of classes. No student had ever done that for us before, nor has any student done that since. It's not that Mike has a lot of money. He just cannot do enough for other people.

If you would like to get a glimpse into the thinking and heart of this great man, look up just two of the books he has authored. Both books will also show his love for and knowledge of the Word of God: *The Old in the New/Shedding Light on Ancient Quotes Used by New Testament Writers* and *Is It Fake, or Is It Real?/Teaching for Meaningful Results*. Those wishing to learn to play congregational music should read *Hymn Playing: Step-By-Step Instructions in Learning to Play for Church*. These books will be quintessential resources for any preacher or music teacher who desires to be effective in serving the Lord.

VIGNETTE 22

THE MASTER OF MIRACLES

THE FOLLOWING vignette demonstrates how the Lord seems to delight in starting with what seems impossible and working all the details out to His glory and praise. Juan Marcos Martinez came across our path when we first went to Monterrey, Mexico to try to help establish a Spanish Christian university. His vignette begins in 1998. Flora Jean and I were in Monterrey in 1996 when everyone thought the university in Mexico was just a dream and would never be a possibility!

Flay Allen mentioned in "A Sixty-Year Friendship" that he went to Mexico in 1998 to help establish this dream. What he neglected to say is that Dr. Carl Herbster was one of the primary forces behind the university project. As the buildings were being built, I was visiting Pastor Herbster in his church in Kansas City and talking about how everything was progressing. We called Flay in Spain and asked him to seriously consider leaving his church in Spain in order to move to Mexico for one year (which turned into two years) for the purpose of starting the university. This began a chain of events that has culminated in helping to establish an outstanding music program at *La Universidad Cristiana de las Americas* (UCLA).

Rejoice with us as you read what God has accomplished in the life of Juan Marcos as he is serving his Savior in his native country:

It was 1998, in Monterrey, Mexico, and I had just finished high school; it was time to go to college, but I didn't have a college to go to. I was blessed by being born in a Christian family; my father, as a matter of fact, had been in the ministry full-time for almost 30 years. Guided by the Lord, our church had started a Christian school that taught K-12, which I attended. However, our school was not certified by the government, being a Christian school with a Bible-based curriculum (from the US); and so I did not have the papers that would allow me into any university in Mexico. But there was an even bigger challenge.

Ever since Jesus Christ saved me through faith in His work on the cross on my behalf (1991), He had changed my attitude toward music: from indifference (I had been taking piano lessons since age 5 and hated practicing) to a burning desire to learn, to compose, and to improvise. So in my mind there was the idea that perhaps the Lord might want me to dedicate my life to serve Him through music, and therefore my plan evolved into a desire to study music in a Christian university. The challenge was the fact that there were no Christian universities in Mexico. Even if there were, I would not be allowed to study there without the proper certification.

So not only was I missing the papers to study in my country, I did not think that was what the Lord wanted for me. I assumed that He would provide for my education in the United States. I was so convinced that in 1997 I told my students (I interrupted my high school studies and taught 4th and 5th grades in our church school due to lack of teachers) that I was going to study in a Christian university in the United States. To this day I am amazed at the confidence the Lord put in my heart concerning my studies. I had nothing to go on but His promise to instruct me, guide me, and teach me in the way which I should go. After contacting several Christian universities, they all informed me that they did not have any scholarships available but that I was welcome to enroll if I brought with me several thousand dollars. That was definitely not a possibility for me. The Lord was teaching me that just as music rests are necessary where there seems to be nothing going on, in life there are also rests where there seems to be nothing going on. The rests in life (and in music) often-times serve to increase the expectation for what follows, and we must observe those rests and wait until the time is right, until it is His time.

The year I graduated from high school I was notified of a Christian university that was about to start in Monterrey! I was confused, excited, and surprised. This was definitely not what I expected or what I had been praying for, but we know that His ways are not only different from ours, but rather they are higher, more excellent. They said they would accept my studies since a person from the board (Dr. Sam Horn) had used the same Christian education system I had. This Christian university was started in col-laboration with some American churches and would not provide the students with certification from my country but would give a certification from a Christian university in the United States. Therefore, accepting my high school papers from an American Christian education system was no problem. "Well, Lord, what should I do?" I asked. The university offered five majors, and music was not one of them, though pedagogy was; and so the Lord guided me to enroll as a pedagogy major at *La Universidad*

Cristiana de las Americas (The Christian University of the Americas.) I had previous experience in education so it just seemed reasonable.

On the first day of classes we were introduced to the teaching staff, and among the teachers there was an American missionary to Spain that had been invited to teach for a few years in Mexico. He would be our Bible teacher and our music teacher, music being offered as a required course for everyone. His name is Dr. Samuel Flay Allen. For most of the eleven students that formed the student body that first semester, this was their first real music class ever. Dr. Allen asked me to help him by accompanying at the piano during his teaching sessions. He was such a gracious teacher, and a humble man too, with years of music training and pastoral experience.

What a blessing He was to my life! He was very daring and decided that our university students would perform a cantata entitled "The Master of Miracles," and that we would travel around the country performing it in several churches after only five months of rehearsal!!! To my knowledge, none of us students had ever taken voice classes or participated in a choir before. It was quite a challenge to undertake, but he was not planning on taking it all on by himself. He called a friend of his to help him rehearse with and conduct us, one that had been his music mentor and the composer of the cantata: Dr. Frank Garlock.

Now that I know Dr. Garlock, I have no idea how he found time to come down for three weeks and practice with eleven freshmen that for the most part could not tell where "Do" was on the score. There also was the language barrier. Oftentimes we would get the notes wrong and he would say, "*No. ¡Muy malo!*" (No, very bad!) in his very limited Spanish. Sometimes it was hard not to laugh (well, we tried to hold it in, at least until rehearsal was over), but it was his passion for excellence that forced us to concentrate and follow his lead. Eventually we got several "*¡Muy buenos!*" out of him, and that is one special thing about him; he knew who he was working with, he knew what to expect, and he knew what he would be able to get out of us in three weeks. He demanded concentration and excellence while at the same time being reasonable with his expectations.

We did not know what orchestras he had conducted or what choirs he had worked with, and he did not try to impress us with all his credentials. He told us what needed to be done, he worked hard with us, and we were not an easy bunch to work with. He would only be satisfied with our best, and he found a way to get it out of us. He made us work hard and he acknowledged our efforts. As demanding as he was, he found ways to balance his criticism with encouragement. The first time we performed the cantata he directed us, and by the time it was over we could clearly see that the audience had been touched by the message of the cantata. The Lord had shown Himself a Master of Miracles once more, right before my eyes.

One other thing I learned from Dr. Garlock is a biblical view of the music ministry. It is clear to him that music is not a business but rather a means of edifying the Church, meaning Christ's universal church, not only the church in South Carolina or in the United States. This love for missions in the foreign field is evident in his dealings as the head of Majesty Music as well as in his personal agenda. He loves his Savior, and he loves the bride of his Savior. Unbeknownst to me, Dr. Allen had talked to Dr. Garlock about me and somehow got him interested in my music education, because there had been plans for starting a music program at my Christian university. Dr. Allen and Dr. Garlock thought that perhaps the Lord would have me be a part of that ministry. But I would need lots of preparation and training if that was to happen. Being a missions-minded musician, he was interested in the project of starting a music major in my Christian university, and he thought that by helping me he would be contributing to the realization of that vision.

Dr. Garlock asked me if I would be interested in studying music in a Christian university in the United States. I had only been waiting for one-fifth of my life for an offer like that one! Of course I wanted to study music in a Christian university, learn how to use music in the ministry, and help others worship our Lord because He is the only Person worthy of our praise! Suddenly, God's plan started to unfold before me. He was guiding my steps, turning that which was impossible for me into an absolute certainty, and He was using Dr. Garlock for that purpose. Dr. Garlock counted it a privilege to invest in my training.

As we sought the Lord's will concerning this opportunity, the Lord opened doors, my parents gave me their blessing, and I flew to Bob Jones the next school year. I knew the Lord was guiding me to major in Music Education because I was quite sure the Lord would want me to teach others, and it allowed me to get acquainted with other instruments which would prove necessary for composing. Besides Dr. Garlock, other people were willing to contribute to this end due to Dr. Garlock inviting them to participate in a fund for my schooling. My gratitude goes to all of them. They were willing to give of what they could call "their own" for my education, and God used their generosity to advance my training for His work. I really believe the education I received was priceless. Some of my teachers were such a blessing that even after 10 years of having graduated, I still feel the impact of their testimony.

I could mention several instances of how the Lord blessed me through my teachers, but I will tell of only one outstanding example. After the Lord allowed me to finish my undergraduate degree, the Lord guided me to stay for a Master's in music composition. I asked Mrs. Joan Pinkston [Vignette 19] if she would be my composition teacher. She accepted. There are so many ways in which my life was blessed by her dedication and love for the Lord that it would take me many more pages to write about them, but I want to highlight two facts: 1) Mrs. Pinkston had been a student of Dr. Garlock, so I could say that I was a student of Dr. Garlock and I was a student of one of Dr. Garlock's students; 2) Mrs. Pinkston had a lovely assistant that graded papers for her, a beautiful girl with a beautiful smile and a heart for the Lord. As He would have it, years later we got married. After almost 7 years of marriage, two children have been added to our family and there is one more on the way. None of this would have been possible if the Lord had not given Dr. Garlock a burden for missions, for ministering to His church at a worldwide level, or if he had refused to follow this vision.

After finishing my education, the Lord brought me back to Monterrey, Mexico. I am in charge of the music in my church and preach about once a month. I also teach at our church's K-12 Christian school, which has earned its certification from the government. The Christian university in Monterrey did start a music program, and I have been a part of it since 2006. During this time the Lord has allowed me to have students from Spain, Venezuela, Honduras, Peru, the United States, and of course, Mexico. I cannot help but see my ministry as an extension of Dr. Garlock's ministry because of the part he played in my education. I praise the Lord for using me to continue the ministry that others began. To God be the glory forever.

—Juan Marcos Martinez

VIGNETTE 23

GOD'S SOVEREIGNTY OVER THE AFFAIRS OF MEN

ON JUNE 1, 2015 I received one of Ron Self's weekly missionary information emails. This particular email really got my attention because it fits right in with the message of the vignettes that are in this book. As you read what Ron has written, I believe you will see that God was working and all that Ron and his wife Chris had to do was just show up.

However, I think I need to inform you of the many years of sacrifice that these missionaries have had to make in order to just show up and serve the Lord in Buenos Aires, Argentina for 35 years. They had their home robbed at gun-point on February 6, 2011. Chris, who was home alone, was brutally beaten by one of the intruders at that time. Their lives have been in the kind of danger numerous times that would ordinarily have driven less-dedicated people off the mission field.

Another incident I am thinking about happened in April 2011 (Good Friday) when a motorcyclist pulled up alongside their car. He had a gun and demanded money. (In Argentina, if you don't comply, the thief will shoot through the car window.) Ron and Chris gave him all the money they had, but he also demanded their jewelry as well. Rather than just drive off after they gave him all he asked for, the motorcyclist shot through the door of their car. The bullet went through one of Chris's legs and lodged in the other one. Getting medical attention for Chris was also a major problem. But God has proven faithful through every circumstance, and Ron and Chris have remained true to Christ.

Flora Jean and I met Ron and Chris when we were in their church for a music conference in 2006 with the Allens. In fact, that year was when they started the music school that Ron mentions in his testimony. We felt an immediate kinship with the Selfs, and we have been friends ever since. If you have read *I, Being in the Way*, on page 34 you will read that a couple of missionaries were staying in our home in Greenville while Flora Jean and I were in Mexico. That was Ron and Chris Self as Ron was at BJU working on his doctorate that he received in May 2013.

God has abundantly blessed the Selfs ministry in Buenos Aires. Crowded church and inadequate parking made it necessary to begin two main Sunday services. Music has also continued to prosper. Their school reached a total of 52 students this year, and the church orchestra totals about 25. Leadership training continues to be a key part of their ministry. Both Ron and Chris teach regularly in their Bible College there in Buenos Aires, along with administrating the overall program.

Below is the testimony by Ron Self:

> It is always a delight to see God demonstrate His sovereignty over the affairs of men, doing things that we could never design or imagine. It seems as if God takes many "strands" and weaves them together in a way that gives all the glory to Him. One of those works of God "came together" in our church today. Hopefully you can see God's hand in all of this and give Him the glory with us.
>
> Strand #1—In the late 1980's our church invited Ken Rudolph to be our speaker at camp. That began a long-term relationship with Ken, who has come to Argentina

8 or 9 times to minister to our people. Ken has a son, Richard, who has gone to Germany as a missionary, where he is presently serving the Lord. God would eventually lead Ken to do missionary work in Germany as well.

Strand #2—Beginning in the year 2000, we hosted a series of construction teams from the U.S., who helped us build church buildings for our five daughter churches. Eventually, the Lord provided us with a number of our own builders, who have now participated in four construction projects in Argentina along with another being planned at this time. Last summer, our builders became aware of a construction project in Germany that both Ken and his son Richard were involved in. As a result, three people from our church went to Germany and helped with a construction project.

Strand #3—A little over ten years ago, as a result of our ministry, a young man named Matías came to know Christ as Savior and began to attend our church. Seven years ago, he came to the conviction that God had called him into full-time ministry. During the past seven years he has taken classes in our Bible College, has led our high-school-age youth ministry, and was recently married to Loida, a young lady who grew up in our church. After our construction team went to Germany, they gave a great report on the work in Germany and their small part in it.

The Lord used all of these events in the lives of Matías and his wife Loida. On Sunday they shared with our church family that they believe that God is leading them to go to Germany as church-planting missionaries! We are very excited about what God is doing, and it is amazing to see how God used so many people who were simply obeying God in various ways, to bring this about in the lives of Matías and Loida!

—*Dr. Ron Self*

I believe we should pray that God will lead other young people to dedicate their lives to Christ just show up and do as Ron and Chris Self have done.

VIGNETTE 24

REVEALED RELIGION

ON MARCH 19, 2015, the Bob Jones University Museum and Art Gallery held an informative lecture called "Revealed Religion." The lecture was in the War Memorial Chapel at Bob Jones University where I studied and learned much of what has guided me through the years.

I attended the lecture that was advertised in the following way: "The seven paintings that hang in Bob Jones University's War Memorial Chapel are the largest assemblage known of works by American ex-patriot Benjamin West. Accompany John Nolan, M&G curator, on an insightful look at the subject matter, history, and artistry of this fascinating and rare collection."

I was captivated by the presentation. Mr. Nolan gave exquisite information and details of both the paintings and the chapel in which they are displayed. The seven imposing and majestic paintings are: *Esau and Jacob Presented to Isaac* (72 by 101 inches); *The Brazen Serpent* (148 by 115 inches); *Isaiah's Lips Anointed with Fire* (150 by 61 inches); *Christ Coming Up Out of Jordan* (148 by 115 inches); *The Ascension of Our Lord* (211 by 114 inches and hangs at the front of the chapel); *Peter Preaching at Pentecost* (148 by 116 inches); and *Moses and Aaron before Pharoah* (148 by 115 inches).

It was mind-boggling to realize that seven of the original eighteen paintings by Benjamin West (six are lost) are now displayed in the chapel at BJU. The Bob Jones chapel is almost the exact size of the proposed Windsor Chapel (50 by 100 feet) where they were originally to be hung. That chapel at the Windsor Castle was never built. Through another series of unusual opportunities, Dr. Bob Jones Jr. was able to purchase this extremely rare collection of seven magnificent paintings in 1962. The acquisition was made through funds provided for that purpose by a friend of the University who asked to remain anonymous.

A booklet with the title "*Revealed Religion*" that may be obtained from BJU for a minimal price, contains the following paragraph: "Painted by an American Quaker under commission of a British sovereign and intended for a chapel of the established church, it seems strangely appropriate that they should finally come to hang in a nondenominational American institution that draws its student body from around the world. As straightforward illustrations of Scriptural incidents, they are particularly suited for the chapel of the 'World's Most Unusual University,' which stands without apology for the old-time religion and absolute authority of the Bible."

My interest in this unique chapel goes beyond these special facts. A good personal friend of mine, Mel Stratton, (who passed away in 1994,) made and designed the frames that now adorn the beautiful paintings. In 1949, I took "New Testament Survey" in this chapel and sat next to Bob Kendall who became an evangelist. His son, Tom, was my medical doctor for many years. There was a beautiful fresco that adorned the front wall of the chapel at that time [see figure 5]. That fresco was painted by Lawrence Saint (1885-1961), one of the most prominent stained-glass artists of his day, whose work is still featured in the Washington National Cathedral.

I led the congregational singing all over northern New Jersey for Mr. Saint's son and gospel artist, Phil Saint, when I was a teenager in the 1940's. Phil used "chalk talks" as a way of sharing the gospel in his meetings. I played my junior recital on the trombone in the BJU chapel in 1951, and our daughter Gina was married there in that beautiful setting in 1985.

Anyone who ever visits the University should take the time to see or tour the War Memorial Chapel just off the "Fountain Square" on front campus. Purchase the little booklet called "*Revealed Religion*" and then take the time to meditate on the biblical stories that these beautiful paintings picture so graphically.

VIGNETTE 25

INTERNATIONAL BRASS QUARTET

TOM CHAPMAN Jr. is the son of missionary Tom Chapman Sr. who has been serving the Lord in Chile for many years and who was my student at BJU in the 1960's. Tim Chapman, one of Tom Sr.'s other sons, is serving as an evangelist in Peru. David, another son, has served at UCLA, the Christian university in Monterrey, Mexico. Currently, David is serving in the music program at Faith Baptist Church in Taylors, SC.

I received the following email from Tom on March 23, 2015. The brass arrangements that Tom mentions in the email were part of a series of arrangements (called *The Sacred Brass Quartet*). I published the series in 1964 (62 years ago) under Sacred Brass Publications. It is amazing to me that these arrangements that I wrote in the 1950's are still being used by the Lord to bless His people internationally. Here is Tom, Jr.'s email to me:

> Dr. Garlock,
> I thought you might enjoy seeing this. This past weekend I preached a music conference at a church in Monterrey. One of the special music groups was this brass quartet that played a couple of your arrangements—"Bringing in the Sheaves" and "And Can It Be." A neat thing about it was that the four of us represent Mexico, Peru, Canada, and the US.

Thank you again for the use of so much music from
Majesty. We use it regularly, and your ministry through
music continues to be a blessing to and set a standard for
many in the Hispanic world.

—*Tom Chapman Jr.*

I believe the phrase "just show up" fits here. At the time I wrote
these arrangements, I was either using them to get Eastman School
students to come to services where they could hear the gospel, or I
was writing them for Christian brass players to encourage them to
use their talents for the Lord.

VIGNETTE 26

A Wonderful Gift

THE FOLLOWING testimony came from Dennis Flower in his March 2015 prayer letter. I use it here to encourage parents to make sure their children get some music training when they are young. What Dennis says about his parents illustrates how important it is that we understand that God is always working in our lives, even when we are not aware of it. I all too often meet people who say: "I studied an instrument when I was young, but then I wanted to quit and my parents let me. I wish so much now that I had stayed with it." I am going to include Dennis's comments here just as Dennis wrote them:

MUSIC MINISTRY — Years ago, when the Lord called me to preach after my sophomore year in college, I thought that was the end of years of music training—14 years in fact of constant practice! Boy, was I mistaken about that! Although the preaching of the Word has always been our main emphasis, the Lord has allowed me to put those years of training to good use on the mission field. So many churches here in Spain and elsewhere lack someone who can accompany the congregation as well as a choir or someone who can even direct a choir.

You might ask, how did it happen that you arrived on the mission field with your music training? I owe it to my parents, who said when they married that if the Lord gave them children, they WOULD learn to play the piano. And when their children came, they backed those words up with discipline and sacrifice. They prepared for me (and my siblings) an open door that one day I could enter and serve the Lord. How grateful I am for that wonderful gift!

—Dennis Flower

Dennis and Ruth Ann Flower (also known as Toodie) have been missionaries in Spain for over 43 years now and they have also translated more than 600 Majesty Music songs into Spanish. They were also very much involved as editors of *Himnos Majestuosos*, the Spanish hymnbook that Majesty Music helped produce for Faith Christian Missions in 2004. This hymnbook that is being used in many Spanish-speaking countries required a second edition in 2007, a third "revised edition" in 2011, and a fourth edition in 2016.

Dennis was one of my students in sophomore music theory in 1962/63—53 years ago, and it is exciting to see how the Lord is still effectively using him and his wife in Spain. His brother, Lance, has taught piano and music theory at BJU for over 40 years. Ruth Ann's sister, Janet, has taught science for more than 40 years as well.

I believe there are two principles at work in what Dennis has written. Number one is the biblical principle that God has ordained for children to listen to and seek the advice of their parents in all they do. God promises a special blessing to children who obey their parents (Ephesians 6:1-2).

The second principle is that it always pays to develop any talent that the Lord has given us. I believe the Lord delights in using whatever abilities He gives us if we will let Him use them in His timing. We quite often never know when that will be. So often we come to the Lord and ask Him to bless what we have worked out. Someone has jokingly said, "If you want to hear God laugh, tell Him your plans." Whether or not that is true, I believe we must come to the Lord and say, "Lord, if You will show me Your will, I will seek to do it with all my might!" As Romans 12:1-2 promises: "That ye may prove what is that good, and acceptable, and perfect, will of God."

Just to demonstrate the second principle, I received an email recently from the Flowers telling of the ministry they have right now in Spain. Since last September, they have been traveling each weekend two hours away from where they live to the Calvary Baptist Church (Iglesia Bautista Calvario) in Valencia, Spain. This is a city of over one million with very little witness for the Lord. The towers of dead churches are on top of the old hills and the people are in darkness. Thirty-five years ago, Dennis led the man to the Lord who is now the pastor of that church. That pastor is now asking the Flowers to help him with his ministry.

This ministry began with Dennis teaching a Church History class to the people. Next, the people asked him to start a choir program. He and Toodie were then asked to plan and direct a Christmas program that was followed by an Easter program. And as if that were not enough, Dennis preaches every other Sunday in the church and teaches a Sunday School class as well.

When the Flowers finished their ministry in Valencia, Dennis was asked to pastor and preach for Alberto Zermeño for five weeks while Pastor Zermeño was in Monterrey visiting his family. They were also working on a new Christmas program for the Spanish-speaking people. It is a delight to know that Dennis and Toodie Flower have followed the Lord's leading. Praise God for the effective ministry that He has given them in a country that needs the gospel so desperately.

VIGNETTE 27

THE TRINITY ILLUSTRATION

FOR MANY years, I have used the overtone series, a natural phenomenon that God placed in sound, as an illustration of the Trinity of the Godhead. This arrangement of tones is the basis for all music the world over. No matter how differently the various cultures of the world are, their music all uses the same tones. It doesn't matter where one starts in the series [see figure 6a], tone numbers 4, 5 and 6 always form a major triad that is contained in the fundamental tone on which the series is based [figure 6b].

From that starting point, it is easy to explain how each one of the notes in the triad can stand alone while at the same time being a part of the triad. Every triad comes from the fundamental note that has all three notes in it as overtones. I use Romans 1:20 to show that I have just given the best illustration of the Trinity of the Godhead that I have ever heard or seen.

On March 11, 2010, I received a note from a man named Richard Kraus in Wisconsin saying how he was able to use this Trinity illustration to witness to a piano tuner.

> I recently had my piano tuned in my home. Using the chords [the triad], I showed the Trinity to the piano tuner who wanted to know more. Before he left, he accepted Christ as his personal Savior.
>
> —Richard Kraus

As far as I know, I have never had anyone tell me in the more than fifty years that I have given that illustration that they have been saved because they heard that truth. Evidently God used this fact of the nature of sound in the heart of one of my listeners years ago. Richard Kraus was able to use this music principle to speak to someone who understood the overtone series. God used His own creation as a bridge or a steppingstone to bring someone to a saving knowledge of our Savior.

If anyone reading this has never heard this principle, may I suggest that you obtain a copy of my DVD set called "The Nature of Music" from Majesty Music, 733 Wade Hampton Blvd., Greenville, SC 29609. The overtone series is explained in detail there.

VIGNETTE 28

THIRTY-NINE YEARS LATER

THE FOLLOWING event is what inspired me to write this book. Cleveland, South Carolina is not even a town. It is just a wide spot on Highway 276 that runs through small towns like Travelers Rest, Marietta, and then further North in South Carolina.

Faith Independent Baptist Church there in Cleveland [see figure 7] invited me to come and speak for a weekend meeting. Pastor John Griffith wanted me to know that it is only a small church. I told him that I like small churches because then my mistakes are small. People always laugh when I say that but I do not mean it as a joke. When a situation is small, it is a lot easier to correct mistakes than when the situation is large. (I am thinking of a political figure who started out as a community organizer so that his mistakes there were small. When he became a senator, his mistakes there were larger. However, when he became the president, his mistakes were gigantic.)

When Flora Jean and I arrived at the church on Friday afternoon, April 12, 2013, the pastor met us at the door with this greeting: "I am so glad to have you here on my 39th anniversary!" To which I replied: "What anniversary is that?!"

I will never forget what he said next: "Thirty-nine years ago today, I was a student at Clemson University. I had long hair. I was into drugs, alcohol, and all kinds of sin. I went to a church in Rock Hill, SC to hear you speak. I trusted the Lord as my Savior that night and now I am the pastor of this church!"

The following is John Griffith's testimony:

I had gone to Clemson in the Fall of 1972, and it was a "party year." However, you cannot seriously study and party at the same time, so I dropped out at the end of that freshman year. I returned home to Rock Hill, South Carolina, to a job I had had in high school and continued the party lifestyle. Things were getting darker with time.

My oldest brother, Frank, was in Frank Garlock's Sunday school class at Southside Baptist Church and asked prayer for me—that is the key to my story! In February 1974, I was in a bar (a converted gas station), it was a "prodigal son" moment, wherein "I came to myself." I became aware of the fact that the music was controlling my emotions and conversations, that the people I was with were not truly my friends (we were linked only by our pursuit of highs), and that the place stank! I realized my life was going nowhere but downhill!

In March, my brother Frank made a special trip to Rock Hill to give me a flyer about Dr. Garlock's speaking at Trinity Baptist on Cherry Road for three nights of meetings and asked me to go. Now, I did not know Frank Garlock or anyone at that church, but the Lord (in answer to prayer) had prepared me to go . . . and I did! That was a miracle! I attended all three nights and on the 3rd night went forward at the invitation. Jim Guber took me to a mop closet and down the "Romans Road." I prayed to be saved that night! When I left that closet, I knew things were going to be different! I returned to Clemson that summer in 1974. I had a brush with a cult, but (due again to my brother, to prayers on my behalf and also to Dr. Joe Henson) I escaped that! Then I joined a group at Clemson (The Forever Generation led by Rich Kerns) and started attending Southside and the CSC Sunday school class there. Everything changed in my life.

The Lord Jesus Christ answers prayer, and I AM GLAD YOU SHOWED UP!

—John B. Griffith

Pastor Griffith's church is a small one but the people really love the Lord and are eager to serve the Lord under their pastor's leadership. Incidentally, the church in Rock Hill was also a small church. I probably went away from that meeting wondering if God had accomplished anything. God was just letting me know that *He was there*, and He was doing what needed to be done as I just showed up. He was working and blessing my efforts for Him, even though I did not hear about it until thirty-nine years later.

VIGNETTE 29

THREE REMARKABLE FRIENDS

ONE OF the extraordinary things that God has brought across my path over the years is the friendship of remarkable people. I have never felt worthy of many people whom I count as friends. I have to recognize that it was God Who brought such phenomenal people into my life, often just when I needed them.

One of these close friends was probably the original impetus for writing this book: Dr. Dwight Gustafson, the Dean of the School of Fine Arts for forty-three years at Bob Jones University. He was born in April 1930, I was born in August of the same year, and he passed away on January 28, 2014. I first met "Gus," as he was always affectionately called, when we sat next to each other in sophomore Music Theory as students. He was always a much better student than I was. However, I believe we motivated each other to develop the talents that the Lord had given both of us as we learned to use them for the Lord even back then.

As I was writing my autobiography in 2011, "Dr. Gus" was working on a book of his own, and he sent a copy of the original draft to me for any suggestions that I might have. Reading Dwight Gustafson's *A Brighter Witness*[1] again recently convinced me that perhaps I should write a book about personal events that have been a part of my life, just as he did. The University Press decided to not use what I said about this man for the back cover of his book, but I still wish they had:

Every once in a while, one comes across a jewel written from the heart and not from the head. "A Brighter Witness" is one of those rare jewels. In these essays by Dwight Gustafson, he lets the reader get a glimpse into his heart and soul through the many and varied experiences that God has allowed him to have.

I knew Dwight for over 65 years. I have never known a more consistent Christian in whatever responsibilities and opportunities God has given him: as a scholar, an educator, a singer, a conductor, a composer, an administrator, an artist, and best of all, a good friend for all of these years. What stands out best in these essays is the meticulous manner in which God is given the glory for every facet of the life of this dedicated man of God.

Dr. Gus had an editor who helped him with his book, Dr. Ron Horton, who has a PhD in English from the University of North Carolina. I, too, have an editor on whom I rely whenever I attempt to write. This person is one of my most remarkable friends. The Lord brought her across my path when I needed someone to help me write books about music that made me look as if I knew what I was doing. That lady's name is Dr. Grace Collins Hargis of the Bob Jones University Division of English Language and Literature. This outstanding scholar has a PhD in Linguistics from Indiana University, among her other accomplishments. She epitomizes what I said about Dr. Susan Kindall in another vignette [#16]: "She is one of the smartest people I have ever met, but her wisdom enables her to carry that intelligence with humility."

Grace has been the skillful editor of every book and pamphlet that I have written during the last 45 years or so: *The Big Beat: A Rock Blast* (1970); *Jesus Christ Superstar: Blessing or Blasphemy?* (1971); *Can Rock Music Be Sacred?* (1974); *Music in the Balance* (1992);

and *I, Being in the Way, The Lord Led Me* (2012). I wish she could have helped edit this book. She has, however, been unable to, due to unforeseen circumstances. Grace knows how to ask just the right questions of an author who is attempting to put his thoughts into words. She has also been able, through her insight and counsel, to help me in all my speaking engagements for the last 50 years. (I went to her for help before I ever began to write.) Her editorializing has always helped me to say things in a more concise way. Her edits have helped to make the musical and spiritual concepts I was presenting more understandable to the average person.

Grace has always enjoyed figuring out how things work. A specialist in the history and structure of the English language, she has also had opportunities to find structure in the sounds and grammar of many languages from around the world. She and her husband Jim, a retired textbook illustrator at BJU Press, are active members at Faith Baptist Church in Taylors, South Carolina. She sings in the choir, teaches a women's Sunday school class, and helps with the *Freedom That Lasts* ministry.

I want to use just a few quotes from the *Vintage*, the Bob Jones University 2015 Yearbook that was dedicated to Dr. Hargis. These quotes help show why I have chosen to single her out as one of the most remarkable people I have ever met. The first two words that are used to describe her in the dedication are "accomplishment and character." The last sentence is a quote by Dr. Ron Horton who is mentioned above regarding Dr. Gustafson: "Grace is a Christian professional, a superb one."

The yearbook also states that "Dr. Hargis has a huge heart for missions." (This resonates with me, because although I have never been "called" to the mission field, I have ministered directly for the Lord in 50 countries), Grace began the Missionary Linguistics Program at BJU in 1974. Through that program she has helped many missionaries understand the basis of the language in the places where they were planning to minister. In the BJU yearbook, there is a picture of Grace teaching her students that I believe portrays the essence of the character of this remarkable woman. She is doing what I think she loves best, and as the book says: "Dr. Hargis loves her students, and she desires for them to grow in Christ-likeness both in and out of the classroom."

I never sat in one of the classes of Grace Hargis, but I believe she has taught me more about the English language and the importance of using it to communicate truth than any teacher I have ever had. This is just another piece of evidence that God can use you, no matter what your gift.

The third remarkable friend that I want to mention here is another person that God brought across my path 70 years ago. I had known about him since I was 14 or 15. At that time I was singing with the Roseville Singers in Newark, New Jersey. The director of that group and my parents wanted me to take voice lessons from an opera singer. This famous singer lived in South Orange, New Jersey, just a few miles from our home. They were thinking that since I was singing with a semi-professional group, it would help my voice to develop if I took lessons from a professional singer. That possibility never materialized.

However, in God's timing, the Lord brought that same singer, Jerome Hines, across my path. In 1997, Mr. Hines came to Pensacola Christian College to perform the role of Christ in an opera he had written and performed 93 times all over the world. What a joy it was to work with him on his opera, *I Am the Way*. It is based on the book of John, which is the book that brought Jerome Hines to Christ; and it was my privilege to conduct that opera with him singing the part of Christ. All the other major singers in the opera performance were men that he had personally led to the Lord.[2]

At that time, I was 67 and "Jerry," as all the other singers called him, was 77. The ten-year difference between our ages made no difference, and we struck up a close relationship right away. You can read more details about that in *I, Being in the Way* on pages 128-129. But here I want to repeat part of what was in my other book because that was what I believe knit my heart to this musician and servant of God as we performed the opera that he wrote.

On March 3, 1961, this great opera singer, who sang more performances at the Metropolitan Opera than any other singer ever has, sang at the Presidential Prayer Breakfast. I am including an abbreviated version of what he said as he witnessed to President Kennedy and all the other dignitaries who were there: 130 congressmen, 40 senators, 20 foreign ambassadors, 20 heads of the Pentagon, and many more government officials.

> *I am not here to sing for the President, though it's an honor. I'm here for one purpose and that's to tell you what happened to me eight years ago. I found Jesus Christ. I have learned that blessed assurance is my life. That's what my song is going to be today. We are all spiritual derelicts and panhandlers before God and we can't save ourselves by our works, but by the grace and mercy of God.*

He then sang "Blessed Assurance, Jesus is Mine." Jerome Hines knew that God gave him this opportunity to be a testimony, and he showed up in a bold way to witness for the Lord he loved.

[1]If you have read this and do not have Dr. Gustafson's book, *A Brighter Witness*, published by JourneyForth, a division of BJU Press, Greenville, South Carolina, I strongly suggest that you obtain a copy. The insights that "Dr. Gus" writes regarding all of the arts and how they are integrated will challenge and inspire you to use whatever abilities God has given you for His glory.

[2]I would suggest that any musician, particularly any singer, reading this should try to find a copy of Jerome Hines' book, *This is My Story, This Is My Song*, published in 1968 by Fleming H. Revel Company. He will challenge and encourage you as he opens his heart, just as "Dr. Gus" did in his book. He clearly states in the Preface: "I don't believe in God—I *know* Him."

VIGNETTE 30

A GOLDEN TRIANGLE

THE GOLDEN Triangle is about the person who has been the most important person in my life for more than three-fourths of the time the Lord has allowed me to live. I am writing this on April 24, 2016, the sixty-fifth anniversary of the day I asked that wonderful person to marry me, Flora Jean Fox Garlock. I still affectionately call her "my doll."

I am calling it "A Golden Triangle" after the designation used by Hebrews for the *Shofar*. The Shofar is actually the ram's horn that is translated "trumpet" in the Bible. The principle comes from "The Golden Section." It is the ratio that God used in forming the horn that the Israelites used for all special occasions (Exodus 19:16, Leviticus 23:24, Joshua 6:4, Zechariah 9:14, and so forth). Without going into any details, let me just say here that the natural construction of this "instrument" is based on the Fibonacci Series of Numbers or the Beauty of Numbers in nature [see figure 8a].

The first time I noticed Flora Jean Fox was when I showed up at BJU for my second semester in the fall of 1949, which was the time that she came to school. We were placed in the same voice class, and I was attracted to her right away. I thought, however, that this beautiful, talented, and tastefully-dressed popular girl would never be interested in the likes of a poor boy like me. I only possessed two corduroy jackets and two pairs of corduroy pants. Fortunately, a year and a half later, she invited me to her society outing with an unusual note constructed by actual music. I was unable to go, but her note gave me the courage I needed to finally ask her for a date.

My relationship with Flora Jean has always been based on a triangle, which any engineer will tell you is a symbol of strength. Visualize a triangle—in which she is in the lower left-hand corner, I am in the lower right-hand corner, and God is at the top. The closer we each get to the Lord, the closer we are together [figure 8b]. This has been true for us since Tuesday, April 3, 1951, when we had our first date at a BJU Bible Conference session. We both knew immediately and instinctively that day that we were meant for each other. We both loved the Lord with all our hearts and wanted to serve Him. That's why I asked her to marry me exactly three weeks later, April 24, 1951. We were married on January 3, 1952, nine months to the day after our first date.

Flora Jean was a farm girl from Oklahoma, and I was a city boy from New Jersey. In spite of that, her German Mennonite parents welcomed me to Oklahoma at Christmas time that school year to marry their beautiful, talented daughter, never having met me. I don't care who the boy was, I would never have done that with either of my daughters! But I believe her godly parents sensed that the Lord was in this and they agreed. I must also say that I loved Flora Jean's parents as much as I loved my own parents. To this day I am grateful to them for having her for me. In fact, when we showed up at Flora Jean's house in Okeene, Oklahoma on December 18, 1951, her parents were there waiting on their front porch for us. I got out of the car and said "Hi, Mom," and we were friends until she went to be with her Lord twenty-seven years later.

Flora Jean has always been a pillar of strength for me. Her love for me and her trust in my desire to follow the Lord's leading for us has given me confidence and security in the midst of the trying circumstances of life. When I was the pilot of the airplanes we owned during the eighteen years we flew, she was frightened to death many times. Not only because she couldn't understand what was keeping that plane up in the air, but as I have said many times: "Flying a small airplane is hours and hours of boredom, punctuated by moments of *sheer terror!*"

Over the years of our ministry, we have lived in small apartments, and even in a dirty, bug-infested room that had been the mother-in-law's room of a poor home in Pensacola, Florida. We also lived in a broken-down house in the middle of Rochester, New York while I went to the Eastman School of Music. She was home alone at night in the middle of the city with our two small children while I worked at Kodak from 11pm to 7am to enable me to obtain the education I believed I needed to serve the Lord through music. Over the years as we have traveled, we have stayed in church basements, peoples' home basements, run-down trailer homes, and cheap motels (among other unusual places where we were conducting meetings).

Flora Jean has never complained about the sacrifices she has made in order for us to do what I believed the Lord had called us to do. If you look through songs and hymns that I have written, you will notice that her name is almost always next to mine in the credits for the music because of the musical talents the Lord gave her to improve anything I was trying to write, particularly in the harmonies. She has always been the proficient accompanist for every choir and every congregation I have ever directed. Our musical talents are different, but they complement each other. By working together we have been able, by God's grace, to accomplish things that neither one of us could have done alone. God definitely blessed us as we just showed up where He wanted us to be. By each of us maintaining a close personal relationship with Jesus Christ, we have remained close to each other for over 65 years.

VIGNETTE 31

MY DAD

SHERRILYN JOY, affectionately known as Shelly, whom the Lord brought into our lives on January 23, 1954, has been one of the richest treasures that a couple could ever have. Flora Jean and I had been married for just two years, to the month, when Shelly came. You have never seen two happier people than we were to have this special little jewel come to live with us.

Before Shelly was born, we had said that if our baby were a girl we would name her "Shelly." While working at Kodak, when I was attending the Eastman School of Music, I saw a photo of a little baby named Sherrilyn. So we decided that would be the name for our baby, and we would nickname her Shelly. There was absolutely no way this young couple could know how gracious and kind the Lord was being to us to give us this wonderful and talented girl. Again, we must say God did exceeding abundantly because we as her parents are amazed at what God has done through Shelly. [See figure 9 for the song I wrote for both of our daughters.]

Shelly has been a special blessing to her parents for all these years. She has always been sensitive, considerate of others, and has had a desire to do the right thing. We never had to make her practice the piano. She started playing before she was three years old, and her "practice time" was always a little recital. She would curtsy and bow before every number. When she was interrupted for any reason, she would start all over again with the whole process. At the age of three she even sang a solo on Aunt Beka's (Beka Horton's) television program in Pensacola, Florida.

We went to BJU to teach when Shelly was six. From then on, after she started taking piano lessons from our good friend and neighbor Muriel Murr, none of the other piano students wanted to enter any of the piano contests that Shelly would compete in. They knew Shelly would win!

One incident will illustrate what I am saying here. When Shelly was ten years old, we took her to hear a senior piano recital in the Concert center at BJU. One of the pieces the recitalist played was Mozart's Piano Sonata #16 in C Major. After the recital, as we were shaking hands with the recitalist, we heard someone playing the same piece on the stage better than the recitalist had played it. It was Shelly!! When we admonished her she said, "I just wanted to hear what it sounded like on that grand piano!" She was not trying to show off or insult the recitalist, she was just innocently doing what she loved so much.

What Shelly has written below succinctly tells of the wonderful, quintessential relationship she and I have had all her life. I cried thankful tears of joy when I read what she wrote:

Where do I begin? How do you put the whole world into a small box?

My dad means the world to me. That about sums it up!

Jesus Christ has become the center of my life. My dad has taught me this by example.

Besides the influence of Jesus Christ, I attribute who I am—my values, my beliefs, my worldview, how I think about God, and how I think about others to my dad.

From a young age, both of my parents gave me an unselfish and unconditional love. I remember countless times being out with my dad in a grocery store, at a church, or wherever, and he would give someone who had a need the largest bill he had in his wallet—whether it be a $5 bill, a $20 bill or a $100 bill. My mom would dote on missionary wives and loved to take them shopping to buy a new dress, not just one from a thrift store. Lest you think my parents had an abundance of money, this was not the case. We lived on a Christian school salary and a small part-time church salary.

Almost every Sunday night my parents would invite someone over after church to eat and fellowship with us. We had every preacher and missionary over to our home that time would permit.

My dad spent countless hours, probably three to four times a week, one to two hours a day, helping me practice the piano—counting with me; playing the left hand while I played the right hand and vice versa; making sure I read the notes and not just repeated what I heard; making me start in the middle of a piece when I missed a note or a rhythm, even though I always wanted to start back at the beginning, which was easier.

If I ever got a craving for ice cream or cookies at nighttime, my dad would stop everything he was doing and run to the grocery store. Many nights my dad came and tucked me into bed and spent time talking with me about anything I wanted. He answered so many of life's questions during that special time. We prayed every night for the man I would someday marry, and look at the wonderful man God sent!

Dad taught me how to give of myself to others, even when not having much money or time. He helped me to learn to work hard and put my entire self into whatever I strive to accomplish in life. He taught me to forgive. He taught me to love my husband as Christ loves the church. I have looked to how my dad loves and treats my mom to get my inspiration.

I cannot say enough good things about my dad. He has tirelessly served the church and his family. He has experienced opposition for his stand on conservative music—but has always done so graciously, refusing not to falter.

I love you Dad! You are truly the best Dad I could have ever hoped for.

—Shelly

After Shelly received her Master's degree in piano performance, she and Ron came to work with me at Majesty Music in 1978. Since that time, she has had a part in producing much of the outstanding sacred music that our company has produced over the last 39 years.

Here is just a partial list:
- 37 Patch the Pirate adventures (We have sold over two million, and she is working on another one as I write this.)
- 21 "Songtime" recordings

 6 Solo recordings with Ron
26 Sacred choral recordings
15 Piano recordings
15 Christmas musicals
 7 Easter musicals
16 Choral collections
   Many choral octavos
 3 Hymnals (each one took years to produce)
 8 Volumes of piano & organ music
 3 Piano hymnplaying instructional books
 1 Book that she authored

This list does not convey the time and energy it took to produce the quality that is contained in all the above. For instance, when Shelly did her album she called "Back to Bach Christmas," I was astounded at what she had singularly produced. She was able to take Christmas carols and arrange them as if they had been written by Bach himself. Here is what I said to her: "Shelly, it is great to know you, let alone think you are my daughter!" Again, I just showed up when Shelly needed me, and I am amazed at what she has been able to accomplish, especially as God has used her dedicated talent to be a blessing to people all over the world.

In addition, Shelly has helped Ron organize, build, and execute an outstanding music program at a local Baptist church for over two decades by writing arrangements, organizing special groups, playing the piano, and overseeing all the overwhelming details that are part of running an effective church music program. She has also been a vital part of what we now call MusiColleges (music seminars) that Majesty Music has conducted. Thousands of church musicians have attended and received help for their ministries through all the MusiColleges workshops that have taken place over the last 43 years.

VIGNETTE 32

MY FATHER

I DON'T believe I could find a better title for this vignette than the first two words of what my son, Jon Randall Garlock, better known as Randy, wrote for me. Randy is a tenderhearted, giving, loving, and loyal son. He is a hard worker and has gifts in business and music. He could sell ice to an Eskimo. Randy has a fabulous sense of humor and consistently keeps our family laughing. I must admit that I am embarrassed to print what he wrote, but I believe I would be ungrateful if I did not thank the Lord for what my only son has written. This reminds me of the many times that we have been in foreign countries and the people are so glad to have us there that they insist on doing something for us. My heart says "refuse the gift, you don't deserve it!" But I also know they would be hurt if we didn't accept what they wanted to give. So, here goes! I am printing this just like Randy wrote it:

My father is a truly wonderful and remarkable man, and I am truly blessed to have him as my dad. When I think of my loving father, it gives me a glimpse of what my Heavenly Father must be like. I believe that the most accurate way to describe God is to think of Him as my Heavenly Father. I believe that the actions, words, and deeds of my earthly father give me a real glimpse of what my Heavenly Father is like.

Anyone who knows my father realizes quickly that he is a rare person. He is blessed with much energy and channels it into worthwhile, lasting projects. Dad has always had much drive. When I reached my early teens, Dad left his faculty position at Bob Jones University and started speaking around the country. The music faculty at Bob Jones University all stated that it took three faculty members to replace him. There are people to this day who feel that they never did replace him! The man has exceptional talents and abilities, and he was always completely dedicated to use his talents for God. To his very core, my father has a strong strength of character and faithfulness. Even in his later years, he still has this inner energy to be tremendously useful and helpful. Even at 87 he continues to be a wonderful influence and help to so many people. I admire him so much.

It has always been thoroughly enjoyable to go to any public place with my dad. It is almost impossible to go anywhere without others coming up to him and telling him how greatly he has influenced their lives, their families, or their ministries. This is true all over Greenville no matter where we go. It is also common in airports around the USA, and I can recall many instances in foreign countries too.

Of his many positive attributes, I must place his desire to serve God at the very top. His dedication to serve God then spilled over in all aspects of his daily walk, including a very strong desire to be totally dedicated to my mother. Growing up, I vividly recall Dad telling Shelly and Gina and me that he loved our mother so dearly that they would always be together. We were assured that our family would be strong and secure. What child would not love to hear this from a loving father!!

I recall that my Dad would always accept my friends into our home and made a conscious effort to befriend my childhood and teenage friends. He always said, "Any friend of yours is a friend of mine." What generous love and support came from this wonderful man. I could always count on my dad to support me and assist me, and he was always there with wise advice. He seems to have this uncanny ability to know when to be tough and when to flood you with love. But most of all, he was always there.

I must admit that I approached marriage with some fear and trepidation. It is not the easiest thing to be the son of someone so extremely strong and incredibly talented. I wondered how I could possibly be the husband and father that I had seen in my own father. While trying to be my own person, I was always aware that I wanted to copy his many various and remarkable qualities. This always managed to be a difficult balance for me personally, and I regularly managed to view myself coming up short. It really did not help matters that Shelly was like this perfect child and could really do nothing wrong. And then along came Gina, and she was truly favored by us all. Somehow, I managed to think of myself as the bologna in the middle of a truly unique and delicious sandwich.

It was my real joy to have worked for my Dad for over 12 years. I remember those happy years as the most rewarding and fulfilling of my entire life. I knew that I had some abilities in business that my Dad did not have, and it was a real joy to be able to add to his ministry through my small talents. Playing trombone duets with Dad and singing with him in many churches and conventions and conferences

around the country was truly thrilling. It was not only my
joy to have a part in my father's ministry, but also in the
ministry of Ron Hamilton, a remarkable person himself.
Who has ever had a better brother-in-law than this guy??
Many readers of these words will say that Majesty Music
has been a real blessing to them, but imagine the sheer
joy and blessing it was to have worked for the ministry!

It has always been amazing how many people have come
up to me over the last 40 years plus and have told me
that "your dad is my favorite person," or "your dad has
had such a profound influence on my life." I wish I knew
how many people have said to me that my father has had
a strong influence in their ministry. It is a never-ending,
sparkling clear river of the purest water that flows through
our lives—those lives that have been so very fortunate to
have walked this earth close to my father, Frank Garlock.
The man is entirely godly in all that he accomplishes, and
his accomplishments are much greater and longer lasting
than anyone else I have ever known.

My father, who has seen the light of day for over 87 years,
shines as the brightest star in the firmament, himself, with
an extraordinary brilliance. Thank you, Dad, for your many
years of sacrifice, complete loyalty to our family, and the
wonderful encompassing love with which you have always
embraced me for my entire life. No father has ever done
better.

—*Jon Randall Garlock*

Randy and I have always had a special relationship. It is not that we
have not had any problems (many people have always thought that

our family was perfect). We are human, and that means that we have had to overcome some obstacles along the way. But we have always faced them squarely and not tried to be something that we were not.

Almost 10 years ago, through some unfortunate circumstances as Randy was working on some international business transactions, some dishonest people allowed a foreign country to blame Randy for some problems that arose. Randy could be bitter, but as you can see from what he wrote, he is not. He has lost a lot in a number of areas of his life during this ordeal, but as you can also see from what he says—he is still trusting the Lord, along with us, to work things out in His time. He has been living with us for almost three years now, and Flora Jean and I are delighted to have him with us.

I would be reluctant to estimate how may fathers I have counseled over the last 65 years who would have given their right arm to have the kind of relationship that Randy and I have always had. His mother and I are eager to see how the Lord is going to use him in the future as he surrenders himself to do whatever God wants him to do.

VIGNETTE 33

THE LENS OF GOD

"Don't look through the LENS OF CIRCUMSTANCES
to understand God.
Look through the LENS OF GOD
to understand the circumstances!"

I WROTE a vignette for this book about my daughter Shelly because she is the one who has followed Flora Jean and me in the field of music. However, I have another daughter, Gina, who could have done well in music but decided among other things that she wanted to go into designing houses for her husband, David Greene, to build. God has allowed the Greenes to go through some circumstances that I want them to tell you about in this book. I believe when you read their story, it will help you understand the quote above.

Anyone who knows Gina loves her. She is vivacious, sweet, fun-loving, and is very dedicated to her husband, children, and to us—her parents. Gina is very artistic and knows how to make things look beautiful in any situation. In fact, just this last Sunday, July 5, 2015, we performed "We Salute You, Lady Liberty" from *Bring Back the Glory*, a musical I wrote for the dedication of the Statue of Liberty when it was refurbished and restored in 1988. The full band score for this extended piece of music is eighty-four 16"x10" complicated pages.

In 1986 as I was working on this project that was to be performed by the Wright-Patterson Air Force Band in Ohio and in other places, Gina undertook the enormous task of copying the score and all the parts by hand. (This was before we could do it with computers.) That means she had to try to understand and then copy the various instrument clefs and instructions to make the music clear and readable. That involved over 100,000 notes and another 100,000 instructions. That does not include copying all the parts off individually for each of the instruments, nor does it include the words that were a part of the score. [See figure 10 for just one page of the myriad of details that Gina wrote out so artistically by hand.]

Gina wanted to use one of the talents that God had given her to do her part to help her father do what God wanted him to do. The Lord used her efforts in the 1980's when *Bring Back the Glory* was used throughout the United States to challenge people to do all they could to hold back the forces of evil. I believe that the message of that work is more necessary now than it was when I originally wrote it in 1985.

I would like for Gina to tell you how the Lord has worked in the life of her family during the last ten years. I am including her testimony in this book since I lived through this with the Greenes and just showed up to help them whenever God gave me the opportunity. May anyone who reads this be encouraged as they see how God worked on David and Gina's behalf even when they did not realize all that He was doing for them.

> I used to believe that God's blessing was living the "American Dream." To have a beautiful family, nice house and car, and a secure job was evidence that I was in His favor. I am so thankful that God did not allow me to live that shallow existence; but instead He has crushed and broken me so that I could learn that I have a personal God who loves me more than I can understand and cares about even the smallest details of my life.

To know *about* God and to truly *know* God are two different things. We must experience brokenness to gain a better understanding of Who God really is and what He has done for us. We should always remain desperate for God. Real faith is not made strong on our mountain-top experiences, even though we love to be there. Genuine faith is established in the valleys where it is difficult to see what God is doing and trust Him anyway. Hebrews tells us that "Faith is the substance of things hoped for, the evidence of things *not* seen."

God had blessed David and me with five healthy, beautiful children during our 25 years of marriage. Life had been good, and we were sailing along—enjoying all of the goodness that God had provided and thanking Him for it. When our oldest son went off to college for his freshman year, I began a new journey of experiencing God. I spent a year in faithful, intensive study and prayer. I prayed for wisdom and for spiritual depth for both David and me. I prayed for our kids to not just be good kids but godly ones. These were sincere, tearful heart pleas—on my face, before God.

Then in March of that school year, things changed dramatically for us. Life as we had known it, and we considered normal, turned overnight into experiences that we could not understand. The collapsing housing market began a downward spiral. Our assets became huge debts; people that we had trusted turned their backs on us; friends abandoned us; we lost our house, our cars, our business, and our church. David realized he had engaged in some unwise business practices; but some accused him of things he had not done. God allowed us to go through these trials for our growth.

Our whole world seemed to crash in around us. We learned to cling desperately to God and to have faith that He was sovereign and in control, "working all things together" for our good. We had believed these spiritual truths for years, and now we were forced to live them out. Our family and a few loyal friends gave us the love, support, and encouragement to remain on a spiritual journey that seemed too hard to walk. This valley seemed unending.

In September of the same year, God very clearly opened the door for us to take over Market Square Deli in Greenville, South Carolina. For three years, God carried us while we faced all the trials with the construction business and legal issues. The restaurant was a blessing as I was forced to get up every morning and face the world with a smile when I really wanted to stay in bed and cry. I told David that if all else failed, we could walk to work with no car or money for gas (the deli was close to our house) and have food for our family from the restaurant. The bank was allowing us to live in our foreclosed house so our basic needs for a roof and food were met. You can survive with those two things. It's amazing how we, especially as Americans, think we need so much "stuff"!

During those deli years, God took care of us in so many ways and quite humorously on many, many occasions. It became so ridiculous that we realized how the emotions of laughter and crying truly are closely related! For exam-ple, we desperately needed an audit of our bookkeeping to prove we had *not* stolen money from our own company. This would cost approximately $30,000 which we obviously did not have. An individual who was wanting to prove our guilt was able to advise the IRS to investigate us, and this resulted in a year-long audit/investigation. We didn't know whether to laugh or cry!

It was a huge headache, but God brought an IRS agent from out of town to do the audit. He didn't understand why they had given him our case, causing him to drive a distance, but we quickly learned that it was part of God's plan. You see, he was a Christian. So he and David were able to pray together that God would help them find the truth in the books. This indeed *did* happen; and although it did not convince our accusers of our innocence, it gave David and me the peace to know we had not stolen any funds from the company.

God remained faithful! Oh, there were times that we doubted Him and doubted whether He loved us. On one of the worst days, when I was needing more than ever to sense God's love, He proved Himself once again to me, in a very personal way. Shelly was recording a Patch adventure. She had been working with my daughter, Blythe, on a solo for the CD called "The Kashmir Kid." I did not know what song she was singing and had not heard them practicing. On this particularly difficult day, Shelly brought the CD over to the deli for me to hear. She played the song that Blythe sang, and tears rolled down my cheeks as my own child, at nine years old, sang in her sweet little voice, "Yes, Jesus Loves Me." The timing and message of the song was so very real to me that I will never forget how God met my need at that very moment!!

This was not a path that we would have chosen, but as we look back on it all, we can clearly see the hand of our God working and know that Jesus led us all the way. [See figure 2 for the song that Dad wrote for David and me for our wedding in 1984.] We now understand that our hurts and our disappointments were part of God's design to shape our hearts and make them tender toward Him. God *was* faithful, and we especially praise Him for such a godly family who stood beside us through every challenge. They truly were God's hands and feet to us in those desperate times.

God used our children to minister to us in ways they will never know. Jeff and his wife Tessa, Reagan and her husband Justin, Blythe, Torie and Gareth have all been the richest blessing that any couple could ever hope to have. As they have lived through this valley with us, we pray that each one has learned that the Christian walk is not a life that God called us to live for comfort and ease. We are to share in His suffering, and only in this way can we learn that we can indeed trust the One who died for us.

We are so thankful for the many people that God used to minister to our hearts as we clung to Him when we could not see the Hand of God and we were forced to walk by faith and not by sight. We have truly learned to see life through "the lens of God."

—Gina Gaye Garlock Greene

VIGNETTE 34

"DADDY, WHO IS THAT BOY?"

WHEN RON Hamilton came to Bob Jones University from South Bend, Indiana, our lives changed forever. Of all the young men (and there are hundreds of them) that the Lord has afforded me the opportunity of mentoring, Ron Hamilton has definitely been the most promising protégé that I could ever have asked for. He has gone far beyond me in so many areas that I cannot begin to mention them all. However, the thing that stands out in my mind and heart is that he is one of the most spiritual men I have ever known. I thank the Lord for his consistency, his discernment, and the character that shows through in all he does.

I have titled this vignette after what Shelly said to me after she first saw Ron in the Vespers Choir that I wrote about on page 93 of my autobiography. She was just a sophomore in high school at the time, but because she and I had prayed for the man God would give her since she was very small, she somehow sensed that she had seen the man that she would eventually marry. By the way, although she had to wait several years to see her dream fulfilled, she never changed her mind!

Rather than ask Ron to write something for this book, I have decided to reprint part of what he wrote as the foreword to *I, Being in the Way, the Lord Led Me.* I do not believe I could have found a better testimony about how the Lord has used my limited efforts and expanded them through the worldwide ministry that he has given to Ron Hamilton.

Ron is probably best known as "Patch the Pirate" because of his ministry to children that has gone all over the world and been translated into at least 60 languages. However, he has written so many beautiful, biblically-based and God-honoring songs and musicals that a book about this aspect of his life needs to be written. He is another person who has unusual, outstanding abilities, but whose wisdom allows him to use these abilities with uncommon humility.

I cannot thank the Lord enough that He not only brought Ron into my life as my student, but He gave him to Shelly to be a wonderful, loving husband for my daughter. Through his wisdom and steadfastness, Ron has become like a quintessential grandfather to all my 14 grandchildren and now to my 6 great-grandchildren (with more to come) as well. As William Cowper so effectively wrote—"God moves in mysterious ways, His wonders to perform" [see figure 11]. Ron wrote:

Dr. Frank Garlock, whom I affectionately know as "Dad," has touched my life in more ways than I could convey in just a few brief sentences. When I first arrived in chapel as a freshman at Bob Jones University, there were approximately 15 serious-looking administrators seated on the platform all dressed in white shirts, dark ties, and dark suits. There also was an additional gentleman seated on the platform who was wearing a striking plaid suit jacket, a brightly-colored tie, and a smile as big as the Grand Canyon. When the clock struck 11am, he jumped out of his seat, ran to the pulpit, and began to lead the singing with a level of joy and enthusiasm that was unbelievably contagious. My, how the student body sang and loved every minute of it.

I was hooked. Growing up, I had always felt that God wanted me to be a music pastor; but after that first day in chapel, I finally had a role model—Dr. Frank Garlock. In time, Dr. Garlock became my choir director, my trombone teacher, my Sunday school teacher, and my "here's how to live the Christian life" teacher. He mentored me with boundless energy, compassion, and creativity.

How I thank God for all that Dad has taught me. Of course, he has taught me the greatest lessons by his life. I've seen Dad Garlock repeatedly step out by faith and trust God when he knew it would involve great sacrifice. In the face of very difficult circumstances, I've seen him respond with prayer, patience, and trust in God. I've also witnessed God's mighty hand of blessing on this humble, obedient servant. God was so good to have brought me under the influence of Dad Garlock's energy, joy, love, and passion for God. Dad has faithfully loved and followed our wonderful Savior, Jesus Christ. To the glory of God, Dad has lived his life well, following hard after the Lord Jesus Christ."

—Dr. Ron Hamilton

I think you can probably see why I have left this vignette for the last one in this book. Dr. Ron Hamilton is not only my son-in-law, he is a close friend; and we have worked together for almost 40 years now. I have relied on his counsel in many situations where I needed someone with wisdom to help me make difficult decisions. Ron has been that counselor for me many, many times. My small investment in his life has reaped benefits for me that are far too numerous to mention here.

The words of Jesus that are recorded in Luke 6:38 are usually applied to giving money, but I believe they apply to the blessings that have come to me through this man of God: "Give, and it shall be given unto you; good measure, pressed down, and shaken together, and running over." I cannot thank the Lord enough for bringing Ron Hamilton into my life!

P.S. (POSTSCRIPTUM)

IMUST say that although I still like it, I am not completely happy with my title for this book. My pastor, Dr. John Monroe, preached recently on John 3:22-30 and called his message "John's Swan Song." The Scofield Bible calls it the "Last Testimony of John the Baptist." Either way, the basic thrust of the message was in verse 30 where John says: "He must increase, but I must decrease." Pastor even used the phrase, "God did it HIS way." Perhaps that should have been my title for this book.

However, I have been thinking of all that God has done for me now that I am 87 years old. I can't get away from the story of Caleb and what the Scripture has him saying in Joshua 14. Listed below are several of the phrases that Caleb speaks as Joshua is dividing the land of Canaan:

Verse 7 —"*Forty years old* was I when Moses . . . sent me . . . to spy out the land; and I brought him word again *as it was in my heart.*"

Verse 8 —"Nevertheless my brethren who went up with me made the heart of the people melt; but *I wholly followed the LORD my God.*"

Verses 9-12a —"And Moses swore on that day, saying, Surely the land whereon thy feet have trodden shall be thine inheritance, *and thy children's forever, because thou hast wholly followed the LORD my God.* And now, lo, I am this day four score and five [85] years old. As yet I am as strong this day as I was in the day that Moses sent me: as my strength was then, even so it is my strength now . . . Now, therefore give me this mountain, of which the LORD spoke in that day."

And then the Bible says:

Verses 13-14 —"And Joshua blessed him, and gave unto Caleb . . . Hebron for an inheritance . . . *because he wholly followed the LORD God.*"

As I write this, I am past the age that Caleb was when he asked the LORD to give him Mount Hebron, the mountain that had been the land of the Anakim (giants). It also is where Abraham, Sarah, Isaac, Jacob, and eventually Joseph (Exodus 13:19) were buried, and it is where David reigned (2 Samuel 2:1-4). Hebron is also known as "the place of fellowship" because it was where Abraham and his descendants wanted to be buried as they looked forward to the coming of the Redeemer Who would raise them up (see Hebrews 11:8-22). This is the mount that Caleb wanted when he was 85 years old.

I mention all of this because of what God has done for me in the past and what He is still doing for me in the ninth decade of my life. Read back over "A Sixty-Year Friendship," "The Aierdi Miracle," and "Brother Frank" to see how the Lord has allowed Flora Jean and me to have a part in missionary ministries all over the world, and in this case to the country of Spain. First, God let us help Flay and Margaret Allen who spent 42 years in southern Spain. Then we had the privilege of helping Al and Helga Bonikowsky who spent 42 years in northern Spain. Both Flay and Al received honorary doctorates from Bob Jones University in 2015, in recognition of their faithful ministry in Spain, one of the most difficult places in the world to build a work for God.

The next thing that comes to my mind is how we have followed the ministry of their children, Andy Bonikowsky and Mimi Allen. They were married in 1985, and they have served in the Basque region of Spain for almost 30 years. The last thing is that we are now working with their grandchildren, David and Danny Bonikowsky, who are both having a part in producing this book as they are also serving in the Basque region of Spain. Just as Ron Hamilton, his son Jason and I have made a trombone trio recording called "Three Generations," we have now had the wonderful privilege of helping three generations of missionaries do the work that God called them to do.

Another missionary project that our family has been involved in was helping three daughters of a pastor in Honduras get the musical training they needed to work with several Central American countries around Honduras. When our oldest grandson Jonathan passed away in May of 2013, we established a memorial fund in his name to raise the support to have each daughter go to *La Universidad Cristiana de las Americas* in Monterrey, Mexico for a year. Each of the three girls has now studied there one year, completing the cycle that was established in 2013. Juan Marcos Martinez has taught each of the three girls [Vignette 20].

For Jonathan's funeral I used a part of a poem by William Cowper, one of England's greatest poets who suffered much of what Jonathan suffered: "God moves in a mysterious way, His wonders to perform." I have set the entire poem to music in memory of our Jonathan, and a copy of that song is included at the back of this book [see figure 11].

I am very aware that some of you reading this may say: "You certainly can't say that everything you quoted about Caleb applies to you, can you?!" You are right!

But, certain aspects do apply. For instance, although I am very aware that I am not as strong as I used to be when I was younger, I still walk up stairs two at a time, I still ride my bicycle (even up hills), I still swim, and I still play my trombone, which is extremely unusual for someone my age.

Also, I cannot say that I have wholly followed the Lord all my life. There have been many times that I have failed my wonderful Savior and have not been the servant that I should have been. But I will say this, and God knows my heart just as He knew the heart of Caleb: Whenever I have known for sure what the Lord wanted me to do, I have tried to do it, no matter the cost. Those who know me best, my wife and family, will attest to that fact. I think this is why God has been so gracious to me for so many years.

I certainly don't know what my *next mountain* is going to be, but I *do know* that God has a purpose in keeping me alive this long. And as I said to my students in "God Knows the Future," He has prepared me for each task that I encountered in the past. I know that things I am encountering now are getting me ready for what the future holds. I do want to be like Caleb and say, "Give me this mountain." (I wrote the following song for the senior saints at Southside Baptist Church in Greenville, South Carolina in 1977. I believe the message of the song is still true, and I must apply its principles to whatever mountain the Lord has waiting for me now.)

> *This mountain I shall own, but not for me alone—*
> *For my children I shall claim this promised land.*
> *Because the Word of God is sure, the future is secure;*
> *All the power we need is in God's mighty hand.*

Give me this mountain,
Give me this mountain;
To the land where giants grow—
That's the place I want to go.
Give me this mountain,
This very mountain,
I shall conquer in the power of the Lord.

Another thing that I am very conscious of, as I write the postscript for this book, is that some of you reading this will wonder why I did not include *you* in the book. I am amazed at what I remember, and I am also amazed at what I forget! (I say that my memory is like Swiss cheese: it has holes in it!) If somewhere our paths have crossed and we have encouraged each other, you and I will have heaven to look forward to where we will have eternity to rehearse all the things that God did for us. As Hebrews 11 says several times: "These all died in faith, not having received the promises, but having seen them afar off, and were persuaded of them, and embraced them, and confessed that they were strangers and pilgrims on the earth." That is also why I believe I must finally conclude that my subtitle for this book is correct. I just showed up, and God, in His mercy and by His grace, chose to use my feeble efforts for His glory. I am just the clay, and He is the Master Potter Who does it all!

With a Melody in My Heart,

— *Frank Garlock*

APPENDIX (FIGURES)

Figure 1: Grains of sand enlarged several thousand times.

Figure 2: *All We Have Belongs to Jesus*

Figure 3: *My Song*

Figure 4: *My Life is Thine*

Figure 5: The fresco by Lawrence Saint that is now behind ornate woodwork in the Bob Jones University War Memorial Chapel.

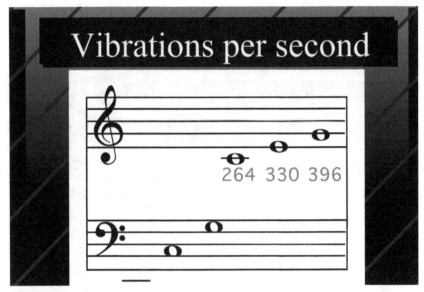

Figure 6a: The first six notes of the overture series that form the basis for all music

Figure 6b: Overtones 4, 5, and 6 that form the triad illustrating the Trinity of the Godhead

Figure 7: Faith Baptist Church in Cleveland, South Carolina

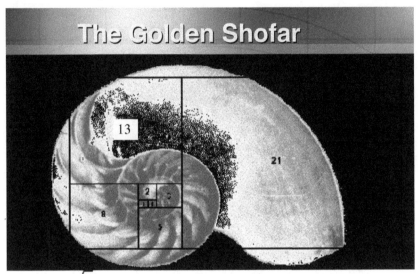

$$\varphi = \frac{1+\sqrt{5}}{2} \approx 1.618\,033\,988\,749\,894\,848\,204\,586\,834\,366.$$

Figure 8a: The *Shofar* that demonstrates "The Golden Section" which is called the "Beauty of Numbers" in nature.

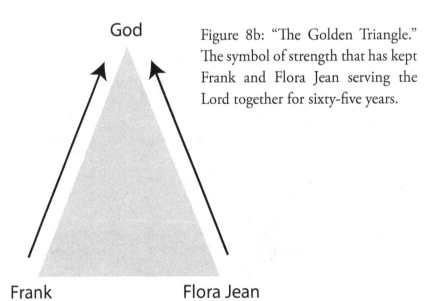

Figure 8b: "The Golden Triangle." The symbol of strength that has kept Frank and Flora Jean serving the Lord together for sixty-five years.

Figure 9: "Our Precious Daughter." Written for the Garlocks' two daughters. ©1998 by Majesty Music, Inc.

Figure 10: *We Salute You, Lady Liberty*. One page of the score executed by hand by Gina Garlock Greene.

Figure 11: *God Moves in a Mysterious Way*